The Best of Judson Cornwall

Other Dr. Judson Cornwall Titles Available from Bridge

The Best of Judson Cornwall

by Judson Cornwall

Published by Bridge Publishing, Inc.

THE BEST OF JUDSON CORNWALL
Copyright ©Judson Cornwall 1992
All Rights Reserved
Printed in the United States of America
International Standard Book Number: 0-88270-665-1
Library of Congress Catalog Card Number: 92-071413
Published by Bridge Publishing, Inc.
2500 Hamilton Boulevard
South Plainfield, New Jersey 07080, USA

Dedication

To Bertie Tholen Jones, long-term editor of *Times of Refreshing*, a faithful minister of the gospel, a great encourager of my writing ministry, and a personal friend of our family.

Preface

One of the outstanding characteristics of the Charismatic Renewal is a tremendous thirst for knowledge of spiritual things. From the beginning of the movement, teachers were in great demand, and books sold almost as fast as a publisher could get them on the market. During the sixties and seventies, many Christian magazines sprung up over the country. As a teacher to the Body of Christ, I was consistently asked to write for these new publications. Only eternity will reveal all that was accomplished through these periodicals. Most were operated on a shoestring, and few remain in publication.

This book is a compilation of twenty-five articles I wrote during those years (1973 to 1991). At first, I did not keep a file of my articles, so some of the magazines are not represented in this book. Of the more than 100 articles I have in my files, I have chosen the ones in this book as representatives. They still speak to the Church in the world.

I have arranged the articles under four headings: The Believer in Christ, in the Church, in Worship, and in Ministry.

I have chosen to use the articles as they originally appeared, with minor editing, although I was strongly tempted to style them with greater uniformity. As you will note, the editorial styles are varied. These inconsistencies, however, do not affect the truths contained in the articles.

I found it refreshing to my own spiritual life to review some of the things the Lord has spoken in days past. It is my hope that these articles will be as vital now as they were when they were written. After all, truth is timeless. It is only the way we express it that changes.

Judson Cornwall
Phoenix, Arizona
1991

Table of Contents
The Best of Judson Cornwall

The Believer in Christ

Christ, Our Life

It has been well said that living the Christian life is not difficult—it is impossible! Only Christ can live the Christian life. One of the most miserable ways to live is to embrace Christian principles without receiving the life of Christ to implement those principles in day-to-day living. Religious people who have never experienced the transforming power of Jesus Christ live with an unresolved inner conflict that induces perpetual guilt and confusion. Like Paul of old, they finally admit, *"For I know that in me* (that is, in my flesh), *dwelleth no good thing: for to will is present with me; but how to perform that which is good I find not. For the good that I would I do not; but the evil which I would not, that I do"* (Romans 7:18-19). Knowledge to do and ability to do are not synonymous.

We are not yet totally spiritual beings; we live in earthly tabernacles and are subject to the pressures of life. But we are at least one-third spiritual beings, and there is a process at work to bring us into an intimate relationship with Christ. *"It is the spirit that quickeneth; the flesh profiteth nothing... ,"* Jesus said (John 6:63). God's Spirit, acting through God's Word and upon God's children, becomes a life-giving force that brings us into the same eternal life that Jesus shares. Being partakers together with His life enables us to be sharers in all that life brings to Him.

The first six verses of Ephesians 2 give us an interesting view of both our position and the process with which we are involved. The first three verses declare that by nature we are (1) dead in sins, (2) confined in the world system, and (3) seated with Christ. Because of God's love and mercy, we are lifted from sin to salvation, from restriction to resurrection, and from being sensually controlled to being seated with Christ Jesus.

"Even when we were dead in sins, (God) *hath quickened us together with Christ,* (by grace ye are saved)" (Ephesians 2:5). The Greek word which we have translated "quickened" is *sunzoopoieo,* which actually means "to (re-)vitalize with, to reanimate co-jointly, to make alive with, or to quicken with." The New International Version translates this verse simply, "(God)... made us alive with Christ even when we were dead in transgressions."

That God made man alive in the beginning is incontestable, for the account of man's creation declares that *"the Lord God formed man out of the dust of the ground, and breathed into his nostrils the breath of life; and man became a living soul"* (Genesis 2:7). Man's life is different in character from that of every other living thing on this earth in that it came as an impartation of the very life of God. Adam possessed more than animal life; he was a recipient of divine life—he had a soul in addition to his body. He was united with God not only in purpose and position, but as a sharer of a common life. He shared the life of God as surely as I share the life of my mother and father.

It was certainly God's provision that this life be perpetuated in the human race, but sin entered, and the consequences of sin—death—replaced that divine life. God had said, *"In the day that thou eatest thereof thou shalt surely die"* (Genesis 2:17). Adam ate of the tree and lost, not biological life, but that glorious divine life that had been breathed into him.

Sin always costs man the divine life that God so yearns to implant within him. The wages of sin is always death, and death cannot have fellowship with life any more than light can have communion with darkness; so before God could bring us together with Himself in Jesus, He had to bring us from death to life, and this He did through the work of Calvary's cross. Christ died not only as God's lamb, paying the ultimate penalty for sin, but He died in our place, as our substitute. Christ died *for* us, and we died *in* Christ. As surely as He vicariously bore our sins, we victoriously share His death.

The workings of death were irreversible, but the finality of death was replaceable. God replaced death with life! Those who came to Christ's tomb to embalm His body soon discovered that God had exchanged life for death. They were questioned by the angels, *"... Why seek ye the living among the dead? He is not here, but is risen..."* (Luke 24:5-6). What God did in Jesus, He does in us. Paul told the Christians in Colossae, *"And you, being dead in your sins and the uncircumcision of your flesh, hath he quickened together with him, having forgiven you all trespasses"* (Colossians 2:13). Here again, Paul used the combined Greek word *sunzoopoieo,* which means "made alive with." We are not quickened apart from Christ Jesus; we become a part of Christ's quickening. It is not a separate life, but the same life that brought Christ from the grave, which lifts us from the death of sin, for we are assured that *"...the spirit of him that raised up Jesus from the dead shall also quicken*

3

your mortal bodies by his Spirit that dwelleth in you" (Romans 8:11).

The Spirit who brought Christ from death to life is now operative in the Church to bring individuals from the death of sin to the life of the Spirit. God is now quickening His saints, and He is giving us the very same life He gave to His Son in order to reestablish fellowship at the highest possible level.

Since this quickening is an action of God's eternal Spirit, which Christ declared was His Spirit whom He promised to send to His disciples, it is not so much quickened persons who live as it is Christ who lives in and through them. We are not simply given life and then told to live it; rather, we receive life and allow that life to live through us. A more intimate basis for fellowship could not have been found.

We live because our *"life is hid with Christ in God"* (Colossians 3:3). We have received this divine life, but it is not sufficient to have received it; we must maintain that life. In the natural, life is received by the action of our parents outside ourselves, but the maintenance of that life becomes dependent upon us. Although God will supply the means, we must apply those means, or the life He has imparted will soon be depleted. The "means of grace" cannot be ignored without the loss of life. Study of the Word, prayer, exercised faith, worship, and love expressed both vertically and horizontally are all necessary means of grace that maintain the life of Christ within us.

Not only have we been quickened together with Christ; God *"...hath raised us up together..."* (Ephesians 2:6), but God reanimated Christ in the tomb and released Him from the tomb, and He is doing the same for and in us today. In declaring us to be active participants with Christ in resurrection power, Paul used the Greek word *sunegeiro* for "raised together." When the Old Testament was translated into Greek, giving us the Septuagint Version, the translators used this Greek word *egeiro* for the opening statement of Psalm 68, *"Let God arise... ."* As I established in my book *Let God Arise*, this statement pictures God arising in order to become actively involved in the lives of the Israelites from the moment they left Sinai until they were securely settled in the land. A very literal meaning of this word is "to stand upright."

We have been conditioned to think of our resurrection as totally in the future, but in the sense of our spiritual resurrection, Paul asserted that it is in the past: "hath raised us up together." At whatever point Christ was raised to stand upright and get involved with life again, we, too, were raised from spiritual death to spiritual life. So radical and drastic is this change that Paul wrote, *"Therefore if any man be in Christ, he is a new creature: old things are passed away; behold, all things are become new"* (2 Corinthians 5:17). Montgomery translates that last phrase as "the old life has passed away; behold, the new life has come."

So unremitting was Paul's concept of the parallel between Christ's resurrection and his new way of living that he affirmed, *"I am crucified with Christ: nevertheless I live; yet not I, but Christ liveth in me: and the life which I now live in the flesh I live by the faith of the Son of God, who loved me, and gave himself for me"* (Galatians 2:20). The Holy Spirit revealed to Paul that the only answer to a sinful nature was identification with the crucifixion of Jesus Christ. We must die with and in Him, for reformation and renovation are insufficient in dealing with the sinful nature; it must die! But this is only one-third of the story, for the Gospel is not merely the death of Jesus, but His subsequent resurrection and ascension. Therefore we

5

are declared to have died with Christ, to have been quickened with Christ, and to have been raised with Christ to be seated with Him in heavenly places. We are now spiritual partakers of the entire work of the Gospel. While there is a finality yet to be received, even the fractional part that we have as a living reality is more than sufficient to enable us to live victoriously and vitally in this present life, for we are declared to be *"more than conquerors through him that loved us"* (Romans 8:37).

Although, admittedly, there were no eyewitnesses to Christ's resurrection, we do have the record of the four Gospels of how the resurrection was discovered, and these accounts, when pieced together, tell the story effectively. The order seems to be that a life-giving energy from God, the Father, pierced the solid stone walls of the sepulchre where Christ was laid and brought new life to the body that had poured out its blood on Golgotha's soil. In this new life, Christ came through the grave clothes without disturbing them, and as the angels rolled away the huge stone that had formed the door to the tomb, He stepped out to allow others to step in and to discover that He was not there.

Is not our participation in Christ's resurrection ordered along similar lines? The pardon for all our sins relieved us of a great load of guilt, but it left us impotent and imprisoned in our form of sepulchre. It wasn't until the life of the Spirit began to course through our beings, quickening us and making us truly "living souls," that we began to deal with the grave clothes that bound us in our tombs. Some of us were shrouded in religious activities, regulations, observances, and rituals, and we found them to be encumbering to the new life that had been received from the Spirit of God. Until we were able to work our way through them, we were very much alive, but as immobile as an Egyptian mummy. Others were muffled and concealed behind yards of winding cloths of guilt, introspection, self-deprecation, fear of unacceptance, and self-pity. They had to learn that the quickening life of God enables them to step through these restrictions without even having to unwind them.

God's method of release is not lengthy therapy; God prefers to impart life that enables us to rise above problems rather than to try to unravel each one through self-scrutiny. If we will move in the life of the Spirit, we can rise above the memories of past experiences and the wounds and limitations of past involvements with life and people. We may be unable to unwrap ourselves, but we can step through and leave the wrappings behind.

God does not give us life and then leave us in the place of death. Once we've learned to rise in newness of life in Christ Jesus, we can expect God to send His angels to open a way of escape. God not only remits the curse of sin; He also removes sin's power to captivate us.

We who once were the victims of sin have now become victors over sin through the impartation of resurrection life into our experience. The door to our tomb has been opened forever, and if we ever enter it again, it will be out of a volitional desire to return to the place from which we were delivered, since an open door allows entrance as well as escape.

It is at this stage of our new experience in God that our friends and acquaintances discover that we are no longer among the dead. They search the old graveyard in vain for our company. When we finally meet them, they cannot help recognizing that something majestic and supernatural has happened to us. While there is much about us that is recognizable, conversely there is much about us that is entirely different. They see that we are living, but they cannot understand the nature of that life. Our resurrection will be discovered, but it will not necessarily be comprehended, for it is unearthly—it is spiritual—and the carnal mind cannot fathom the existence of such life, much less be capable of analyzing it.

The newborn baby doesn't have a clue as to what has just happened to it; it merely lives the life that was imparted to it, until, through the process of maturity, understanding comes. Even so, the "raised ones" of Christ's children need not spend time trying to determine what they have received; they are too busy living as freed individuals who have been brought into a new life in God's kingdom. Fortunately, we do not have to comprehend and understand this life to live it—we merely need to receive it.

This new life we have received as a replacement for our sin-cursed, death-condemned life affects our entire being. Our walk through this world is changed, for we now walk in the Spirit as a preventive to fulfilling the lusts of the flesh (see Galatians 5:16). Instead of living by our animal impulses or our intellectual reasoning, we have the inner guidance of the Holy Spirit, who has raised us to newness of life in Christ Jesus. It is a totally different way of living, for the domination of humanism is replaced by the dominion of the Holy Spirit. We no longer follow the ways of the world; we follow the direction of God as revealed in His Word and as impressed upon us by His Spirit. Our homes become "heavenly places" rather than "the gates of hell." Our relationships with others are founded on love rather than on lust, and even the way we handle our money comes under the guidance of the Holy Spirit.

Those who have been made alive in and with Christ Jesus are told, *"If ye then be risen with Christ, seek those things which are above, where Christ sitteth on the right hand of God. Set your affection on things above, and not on things on the earth. For ye are dead, and your life is hid with Christ in God"* (Colossians 3:1-3). So this resurrection life affects the way a person lives, the way he talks, the way he thinks, and even the object of his affection. This life makes him different from those who do not possess it. It is almost the difference between a stuffed animal in a museum and a live animal in a zoo. Outwardly they look very much alike, but inwardly one has a life-giving principle at work, while the other only gives the outer appearance of being alive.

Resurrection life does, indeed, effect a radical change in our state, but this change does not come through constant striving or disciplined control. This life makes us different—we're "new creatures." We've put off the old man and put on the new; we've enjoyed a spiritual resurrection. We are in the world, but not of it (see John 17:11,14). We've changed locations and are seated with Christ.

Somewhat like Peter and John on the Mount of Transfiguration, or like John on the Isle of Patmos, the people of God have been set in places where the privileges of heaven are enjoyed, where the atmosphere of heaven fills our spiritual nostrils, where the fellowship and the enjoyment of heaven are known, and where an elevation of spirit is experienced as if heaven had already begun for them. We are spiritually seated *"together in heavenly places in Christ Jesus"* (Ephesians 2:6). And if we are seated in Christ Jesus in the heavens, then we are not only *where* He is, but we become part of *what* He is.

It may, indeed, be impossible to live the Christian life, but, on the other hand, it is totally unnecessary. Once the life of Christ is imparted, we are programed to follow the direction of the Holy Spirit quite intuitively, for He has become our inner life, the animating principle of our being. Following His direction is little more than obeying the instincts of our spiritual life. As we follow these inner directions, we, like Christ, will reach out to people in the world who are hurting. We will share the love that has permeated our beings and will offer the wisdom and counsel of the Holy Spirit to those who have lost their way. We will live by His life, and as we allow that life to be lived out through us, we will become the only visualization of Christ the world will ever see. The reason for making us participants in resurrection life here on this earth is to *be* Christ in the world.

God has *quickened* us together with Christ, *raised* us together with Christ, and *seated* us together with Christ. We have been revived and raised, and now reign as regents with Christ Jesus. We live by His life, walk in His life, and reign through His life. God's process is to make us partners with Christ in everything from the cross to the crown.

(From *Times of Refreshing*)

Children of God

Paul was a master at comparing spiritual things with natural things, for he sensed that this natural world was but a foretaste of the world that is to come. He wrote, *"However, the spiritual is not first, but the natural, and afterward the spiritual"* (I Corinthians 15:46). Using this principle, we can discover many parallels between the natural and the spiritual development in a person. As a matter of fact, the recently converted person is frequently called a "babe" in the New Testament (see I Corinthians 3:1). The "spiritual DNA factor" is at work in him, and he will mature into the likeness of his heavenly Father.

The Spiritual Child/Man

Jesus liked to use the child as an object lesson in His teaching. He said that we must become as little children to enter the kingdom of heaven, and that the person who humbles himself as a child becomes the greatest in the kingdom. He even went so far as to declare that *"whoever receives one little child like this in My name receives Me"* (see Matthew 18:3-5).

There is something wonderful about spiritual childhood. While there is so much to learn, there also seems to be a God-given capacity to learn. The curiosity about spiritual things causes this spiritual child to search the Scriptures and to ask questions without embarrassment.

11

The life in the Spirit is almost like a game to him, and his enthusiasm for this new life is boundless and contagious.

He is still very dependent upon others, of course, but every day he learns new areas where he can care for himself. He is already developing very definite likes and dislikes, and his spiritual taste buds prefer some things over others. He enjoys being with the fathers and mothers in the kingdom, but he really prefers to spend time with his peer group, for they think and talk alike. They are still young enough to experiment and play games, while the older Christians are far too serious to be involved in such things. No one takes them too seriously, and they are given virtually no responsibility in the church. They just enjoy life in Christ without any of the pressures that maturity will bring to them. They are children of God—very immature children—and they are enjoying their childhood.

The Spiritual Adolescent/Man

Christians also experience a time of spiritual adolescence—a season when maturity has brought them out of childhood but has not ushered them fully into adulthood. It is a confusing time that often poses a threat to their faith. This is the season of life when rebellion manifests itself, although they are still very much sons of the Father. This is the most likely period of development for the "prodigal son" experience, but a short season in the pigpen usually convinces them that things are better in the servant's quarters back home than in the stinking pigpen. When they do return, they discover that they will be received not as servants, but as sons, for the Father's attitude toward them never changed during their absence.

The spiritual adolescent experiences difficulty understanding some of the changes that are taking place in his spiritual life. He discovers that some of the elementary principles that he had enjoyed as a child of God do not seem to fit all the situations of his life now. He is forced to rethink his faith, and often he must abandon his comfortable formulas and replace them with a more intimate relationship with God. He is being asked to shoulder some responsibility in God's family, and he is striving to be spiritually self-sustaining. It is a difficult, but transitory period in the life of a maturing believer. He is still a child moving into manhood, and he vacillates between the two roles.

The Spiritual Adult

The adolescent spiritual life is often a period of great drive, ambition, and vision, but it is the spiritually mature individual who accomplishes most of the work in the kingdom of God. When John wrote his first epistle, he wrote to "little children, young men, and fathers" (see I John 2:12-14). He recognized that the Church is also called the family of God, and that every age group is to be found gathered together. But while John was willing to address them at their existing age level, the thrust of his epistle was to encourage spiritual maturity.

Although we should retain some of the childlike spirit that keeps us wondering at the things of the spiritual kingdom and simply enjoying being a Christian, there is a call to maturity that challenges us to be like Christ. In his beautiful love chapter, Paul wrote, *"When I was a child, I spoke as a child, I understood as a child, I thought as a child; but when I became a man, I put away childish things"* (I Corinthians 13:11).

A part of developing spiritual maturity is learning to accept some responsibility for spiritual actions. Rev. David Mainse, host of the "100 Huntley Street" television

13

program, tells of a time when he was facing a major decision that would affect both his life and his ministry. He was fasting and praying for God's guidance in the issue when he heard the Lord saying, *"David, you make this decision."*

He responded, "Lord, You've never done this to me in the twenty-five years that I have served You. I need Your will in this decision, not my will."

Unable to change God's mind, he had to make and live by that decision. Fundamentally, the Lord was merely telling him that he was no longer a child who had to receive orders on everything; he was a spiritual adult capable of making decisions for his life. Maturity can be painful, for it demands from us what we have automatically demanded from others.

The New Testament teaches us that we should be like little children, and also that we should grow up in Christ Jesus. Which is correct? Each is! There is value in retaining some of our childlike qualities if we can do so without becoming childish. However, productivity and repro-duction in the Body of Christ call for Christians who have come into full maturity. How can we balance these two extremes?

It is unlikely that we will ever have them in perfect balance. At times, the child will predominate, and at other times the adult will control us. Perhaps we should be content to stay within the limits God seems to have provided in His Word. Nonetheless, our relationship with other members in the Body of Christ is vital. If we seem to be too childlike, fellow Christians will adjust us to a better balance of adulthood, and if we are so serious and mature that we have lost the spontaneous enjoyment of life, they can adjust us accordingly. There is no better adjustment available for an individual than a warm family

14

relationship, both in the home and in the Church. Members of the family tend to adjust the attitudes of one another and to act as safeguards against extreme imbalances. It is little wonder, then, that the Scriptures urge us, *"Let us consider one another in order to stir up love and good works, not forsaking the assembling of ourselves together, as the manner of some is, but exhorting one another, and so much the more as you see the Day approaching"* (Hebrews 10:24-25).

(From *Harvest Time*)

15

The Engagement Ring

Although my granddaughter has been right-handed from birth, she recently walked into our house with her left hand extended, and with a smile that would have melted an iceberg. She had come to show us her new engagement ring. The diamond substantiated her Christmas announcement that she was going to get married. She now had visible evidence that she had made a commitment to a young man, that he in turn had made a lifetime commitment to her, that a complete change in lifestyle was pledged, and that we could expect to enjoy a gala wedding sometime in June.

My granddaughter is not yet married, but the display of her ring has announced her intentions to everyone at work, at church, and in all of her social contacts. She is now busily gathering all the items she will need to set up housekeeping, for her goal in life is not merely to wear a ring, but to become the wife of the man she loves. She is betrothed. Her ring is simply evidence of that betrothal.

When Paul was writing to the Christians in Corinth, he said, *"I am jealous for you with godly jealousy. For I have betrothed you to one husband, that I may present you as a chaste virgin to Christ"* (2 Corinthians 11:2). That we are the betrothed bride of Christ is widely taught in the Bible, but what is so often overlooked is that God has given us an

17

engagement ring as an outward evidence of our engagement, for the saints in Ephesus were told, *"...you were sealed with the Holy Spirit of promise, who is the guarantee [KJV 'earnest'] of our inheritance"* (Ephesians 1:13-14). The Greek word that Paul used for "guarantee"—*arrabone*—is the modern Greek word for "engagement ring." In giving us His Holy Spirit, God gave us an engagement ring to let all heaven, earth, and hell know that we are the espoused Bride of Christ.

We are engaged to Jesus Christ, and we have His Spirit as proof of that engagement! As we display the Spirit in our daily lives, it is evidence of everything an engagement ring depicts.

Evidence of a Commitment

Just as my granddaughter's ring is a declaration that she has made a commitment to the young man in her life, so the presence of the Holy Spirit in our lives is a demonstration that we have made lifelong commitments to the Lord Jesus Christ. Our relationship is more than a flirtation; we have pledged our lives to be lived for Him alone.

In the same way the ring evidences that a young man has made a lifelong commitment to be a loving husband to my granddaughter, so the Holy Spirit's presence in our lives is continuous evidence that Christ Jesus has pledged Himself to be our loving Husband throughout eternity. He will be the Source and the Object of our love. He will provide all needful things during our span of life, and it will be His pleasure to present us before the Father as His chosen Bride when we enter heaven. We need not simply hope for this relationship; He has pledged it to us and has sealed it with the giving of the Holy Spirit. How proudly we should demonstrate the Spirit's presence in our lives!

Evidence of Coming Change

Following the giving of the ring is a ceremony in which a new name is taken by the bride, and she and her groom become one in the union of marriage. The bride leaves her father and mother and is joined to her husband in a totally new way of life "till death us do part."

The presence of the Spirit in the life of a believer is *prima facie* evidence that change is in the near future. The Moffatt translation of Psalm 45:11-12 reads, "Listen, O bride, and bend your ear! Forget your own folk and your father's house; and when the king desires your beauty, yield to him—he is your Lord." Acceptance of the Holy Spirit is automatically an acceptance of a change in living. An old way of life is to be forsaken forever, and a new way of living is embraced. We no longer live for ourselves, but we live for the One whose life we are to share. We trade family relationships and responsibilities. Furthermore, we begin to assemble the things needed to "set up housekeeping" with Christ. We read and study everything about Him that we can find, for we want to please Him above pleasing ourselves. We want to be able to adapt ourselves to Him in every area of life. This is not divestment of personality; it is a deliberate blending of our person to fit into His personality.

The presence of the Spirit in our lives is more than a demonstration that we are going to spend eternity with God; it is an engagement that shows every observant person that we are about to be married and that we will never be the same again. We are surrendering our independence for the greater joy of interdependence with the One we love so dearly. While we may lose the convenience of unilateral decisions, we gain the security of shared responsibilities. We are trading our loneliness for companionship, and our limited abilities for shared

19

abilities which make for a fuller and more complete life. Whatever we may lack in this life of ours, Christ is more than able to compensate for, and He will do so, not as a benefactor, but as our Husband. He has a vested interest in us because He has chosen to love us enough to ask us to become His lifelong Bride. We are even more precious to Him than we have allowed Him to become to us. His love is our security, and His Spirit, as our ring, is a constant demonstration of the depth of His love for His Bride-to-be.

Anticipating is a Time of Joyfulness

If all the hopes and dreams that accompany the giving and receiving of an engagement ring could actually be realized, we would probably live in a perpetual utopia, for hope springs eternal in the hearts of lovers, and the engagement ring becomes a lifelong symbol of promises pledged, dreams pursued, and lives shared. The ring is a beginning of happy anticipation in life.

In most cultures of the world, a wedding is a time of great joyfulness. In our country, the bride is the center of attention at the wedding—it is her opportunity to be "queen for a day." She begins planning for the wedding months in advance, and every detail is carefully mapped out so that the actual ceremony will be a thing of beauty and joy for all who participate in or watch it.

Having given three daughters in marriage and having been an active participant in the weddings of two granddaughters, besides performing wedding ceremonies for many couples while I was a pastor, I have to admit that it is difficult to tell which is the occasion of greater joy— the preparation for the wedding or the actual wedding pageant itself. During the months of preparation, mother and daughter often find a fresh relationship, and friends and family enter into a comradeship at a higher level than before. Shopping, sewing, selecting, showers, and the multitude of other activities that precede the wedding are joyous times of fellowship. It is a brand-new adventure for the bride, and those around her enter vicariously into the newness of life. There are, of course, times of tension and tears, but the overriding joy prevails all the way into the wedding reception, when the guests feast and fellowship in the joy of the bride and groom.

We who are engaged to Christ have come into a glorious joy that will not diminish even after the wedding ceremony. The Spirit, as our engagement ring, is the source of our joy and should be a constant reminder to *"rejoice in the Lord always. Again I will say, Rejoice!"* (Philippians 4:4). We are presently involved in the preparations for the wedding, and we are having the time of our lives. We are not headed for a funeral; we are going to a wedding, and we are the Bride-to-be. Just look at our engagement ring!

(From *Harvest Time*)

21

Introspection

Oftentimes, following the deep dealings of God in our hearts, we find that there comes a turning inward. I want to show you from God's Word how absolutely dangerous this is. Let's look at Psalm 77:1-15. For years, as I read this, I thought it was a beautiful psalm about a man who cried unto the Lord, and the Lord heard and delivered him. Then the Holy Spirit showed me differently. This is a psalm of Asaph, a man who had "I" trouble. As you read these verses, you will see that he was totally self-centered and totally introspective.

Introspection Destroys Peace

There are three things which introspection will do, as we see in this psalm. First, introspection destroys peace. Asaph had a day of trouble. He progressed downward from talking to God to just seeking Him, and he tried to find God in himself, but God wasn't there. You won't find God in you—that is, in your soul, which is generally where you do your searching. God is Spirit and dwells in spirit. Then Asaph only "remembered" God. By the time we reach verse 6, we see the poor fellow lying on his bed at night, unable to sleep, with sores running, no song, remembering the "good old days," and communing with his own heart instead of God.

23

Where most of us get into trouble in this area of introspection is this: As we worship the Lord and are drawn closer to Him, the Holy Spirit begins to shine the light in our hearts, and we see many things we didn't know were in there. But He selects only one and says, "This is inconsistent with the Divine nature and is going to hinder your getting any closer to God. Can we have it?" And we let Him take it. Victory, release, blessing—oh, it's marvelous! But tomorrow our memory circuits begin working, and we remember all the other bad things we saw. So we try to help God out so He won't have to come back and do it, and we go in to remove some of those bad things; but they crush us, and our peace is destroyed. No amount of what we do enables us to get even one bad thing out of our spirit. Man is totally incapable of changing his spirit. Only the action and interaction of the Spirit of God upon the spirit of man can effect any permanent change in man's spirit.

Introspection Questions God

Second, introspection questions God. In verses 7-10, Asaph asked six foolish questions: (1) *"Will the Lord cast off forever?"* Hebrews 13:5 says, *"I will never leave thee, nor forsake thee."* God chastens His children, but has never cast them off; (2) *"Will He be favorable no more?"* Psalm 5:12 tells us that God compasses (crowns) the righteous with favor; (3) *"Is His mercy clean gone for ever?"* Read Psalm 136 and notice how every verse ends— *"for His mercy endureth forever."* (4) *"Doth His promise fail forevermore?"* Note I Kings 8:56—*"There hath not failed one word of all His good promises."* It is impossible for God's promises to fail. Sometimes we think they have failed because we don't understand them. Some of the heavy emphasis we have had upon "faith teaching" says that I am the center of faith and that faith operates so that I can have all things. It says that all of God's promises are mine automatically if I just believe. But that doesn't work. There are conditions to be met. And faith doesn't originate in me, or even in the Bible; faith originates in God and in the word He speaks. Faith is not believing God for whatever I want, but believing God for whatever He says. I may fail in my handling of the promise, but the promise cannot fail; (5) *"Hath God forgotten to be gracious?"* How can God forget His own nature? Grace and graciousness are part of the essential nature of God. He cannot forget Who He is; (6) *"Hath God in anger shut up His tender mercies?"* God's anger is not to withdraw His tender mercies, but to chasten us back into them. God's anger is not from frustration or an inability to cope. It is His fixed attitude toward sin. God chastens not in anger, but in love. To be chastened by God is an evidence of being received into Divine love.

Introspection Leads to Wrong Conclusions

Third, introspection will cause you to draw wrong conclusions. It tends to make martyrs out of us. We morbidly begin to believe that we deserve whatever is happening to us. We start looking inside ourselves to find out what is wrong, and every time we find something wrong we say it's God's fault. Wait a minute! You'll never find anything about God in you. If you are introspectively looking within, whenever you find something wrong, you'll blame somebody else.

The Way Out of Introspection

But there is a turning point! We see it in verses 10-12, and it begins with remembering—remembering God's works and wonders. One of the best ways out of intro-

25

spection is to start remembering what God has done—not miserably (as Asaph did in verse 5), but prospectively. We move from the things God used to do to the marvelous things He is doing now. When we get our minds off ourselves and onto Him, we're already on our way out of trouble.

Then note that introspection is overcome by the upward look. Asaph said, *"Thy way, O God, is in the sanctuary."* This is the holy of holies. God is in the holy of holies and we're only in the holy place, but at least there we can begin to see the ways of the Lord and have an awareness of Him. Oh, how we need to get our eyes off us and on Him and His ways! Don't go looking for sins to confess; let the Holy Spirit be the revealer of what needs to be cleansed. Don't do His work *for* Him; work *with* Him. Let Him take care of what needs to be handled. In the meantime, just stay in the holy place and enjoy Him. That's where His way is.

Isaiah 60 declares that we are to do three things: Arise; shine; lift up our eyes. None of these is consistent with introspection. Introspection never shines; it goes to darkness. Introspection never sees; it just stays awake in the night when nothing can be seen anyway. God's call to His Church now is for us to arise, shine and see. We are to get out of our self-centered, self-seeking concept and see Him; to look at Him so that the radiance of His presence becomes an illumination within; to see what the Holy Spirit shines the light on, and everywhere He goes there is light in the Lord. So rather than be an Asaph who begins as a bragger and ends as a blamer, let's just accept what we have received, and arise, shine, see, and enjoy the goodness of God.

(From *Logos Journal*)

The Ring of Light

At the re-creation of the earth, God's first creative word was " *'Let there be light'* " (Genesis 1:3), and His first creative action was to divide the light from the darkness (Genesis 1:4). That division is as extant today as it was then. Light and darkness do not mix, for light is a positive energy, while darkness is but the absence of light. While light can pierce the darkness to varying intensities, darkness cannot penetrate light in any measure, for light always dominates.

All of us have stood in a storm surrounded by pitch blackness, only to have the whole area suddenly and brilliantly illuminated by a flash of lightening. It was almost as if the light was informing the darkness that it can invade that darkness at will, and when it enters, it pushes back the darkness at the speed of 186,000 miles per second. Darkness has no defense against light.

Similarly, darkness has no offense against light. Have you ever seen a flash of "darkening" that obliterated the light of day for even a split second?

In the New Testament, Satan, his work, and his kingdom are spoken of as "darkness" (see Colossians 1:13), while God is defined as being *"light and in Him is no darkness at all"* (I John 1:5). Furthermore, it defines salvation as an act of God that brings us out of darkness and makes us children of light. Light triumphs in both the natural and the spiritual. We are more than mere reflectors of light; we are recipients of God's light. We both dwell in the light, and the Light dwells in us.

This double provision of light means that we are a double threat to darkness. I have often been asked if I am afraid to go to Third World nations where the dark powers of Satan are so openly displayed. "Aren't you afraid of the darkness?" persons ask.

"There is no darkness where I go," I answer them, "because the light within me pierces the darkness around me. I am like a flashlight on a dark night."

The Word declares, *"You are of God, little children, and have overcome them, because He who is in you is greater than he who is in the world"* (I John 4:4). We are not subject to darkness; darkness is subject to us.

The similes, metaphors, illustrations, and antitypes that light makes available to any preacher or teacher are multitudinous, but among the pictures that light brings to mind is *protection.* We have long been informed that light is a deterrent to crime, and so many of us install outside lighting around our homes.

The prophets recognized this, for Zechariah, in speaking of Jerusalem in the day of her restoration, declared, *" 'For I,' say the Lord, 'will be a wall of fire all around her, and I will be the glory in her midst' "* (Zechariah 2:5).

The context speaks of Jerusalem being so enlarged as to extend beyond her own walls of protection. Since Jerusalem of the Old Testament pictures the Church of the New Testament, this implies that the Church would so outgrow her natural boundaries as to lack natural protection, but God offers the light of His presence as a defense to her. A "wall of fire," or a "ring of light," is the defense God has designed for His people. God need not contest the darkness with His armies; He merely surrounds

His people with a ring of light that the powers of darkness cannot penetrate.

In May of 1984, I was ministering in Singapore in a large convention. One of the other speakers was a precious brother from Scotland who is ministering as a missionary to the Zulu tribe of Africa. He told me the following story:

> The neighbor of a Christian Zulu became very angry with the Christian and determined to have him killed through witchcraft. Stealing a slipper from the Christian's hut, he took it to the killer witch doctor (not to be confused with the standard tribal medicine man) and offered him a substantial fee if the witch doctor would induce the spirits to kill this neighbor.
>
> The witch doctor went into a prolonged trance, but when he came out of it, he said, "The spirits say that they are unable to get through to this man."
>
> Frustrated, and angry with the witch doctor, the man offered him additional money if he would try once more.
>
> Holding the slipper, the "doctor" again went into a trance, seeking to implore the demons to destroy this man's neighbor. After a lengthy period of time, the witch doctor came out of the trance, still holding the neighbor's slipper in his hand.
>
> "Is it possible," he inquired, "that the person who owns this slipper might be a Christian?"
>
> "Why, yes," was the reply. "But what difference does that make?"

29

> "The spirits tell me that the house of the owner of this slipper is surrounded with a ring of light so intense that it will destroy the spirits if they try to penetrate it."
>
> As a direct result of this incident, the godless man with murder in his heart soon gave his life to Jesus Christ. He wanted that kind of protection, too.

God has placed a wall of light around believers as an impenetrable barrier to demonic forces. The Psalmist knew this, for he wrote, *"Because you have made the Lord, who is my refuge, even the Most High, your habitation, no evil shall befall you, nor shall any plague come near your dwelling; for He shall give His angels charge over you, to keep you in all your ways"* (Psalm 91:9-11).

" *'Let there be light' "* (Genesis 1:3) is still God's first word to every new creation. None is saved to struggle against darkness; we are saved to be safeguarded against darkness forever, for *"God divided the light from the darkness"* (Genesis 1:4), and that division is eternal. We may live in a dark place, but we will shine as the stars of the heavens. The spirits of darkness may be commissioned to destroy us, but the ring of light that surrounds us becomes an impenetrable defense for us.

We have been authorized to *"cast out demons"* (Mark 16:17), but the demons have neither the authorization nor the ability to cast us out of the light of God which has shone into our hearts.

We have a ring of light around us, and "God is [that] light."

(From *Harvest Time*)

Practical Christianity

In times of distress, most believers will pay any price for an intervention from God, but in normal seasons of life, they would like to ignore the very existence of God. To millions of people, God is either a luxury or a necessity, but He is almost never a staple commodity of life. People want God on standby as insurance against calamity, much as a corporation engages an attorney on a retainer fee, but it is earnestly hoped that neither God nor the attorney will ever be needed. Most individuals do not want God to be a stationary influence in their day-to-day behavior. "Rescue me, but don't regulate me" seems to be the popular attitude toward God.

The longer I live, the greater becomes my conviction that nobody wants a truly practical religion; people want a "super-natural" religion. Throughout the world, everyone wants a god who can be propitiated when he is angry and petitioned when the suppliant is needy, but on all other occasions of life, it is hoped that this god will stay out of the affairs of people. The greater the distance between the world of the gods and the world of human behavior, the happier the worshippers seem to be. They are content to let certain "specialists" maintain a contact with the gods, and these propitiators are hired when a contact with a god seems valuable or necessary.

This is not characteristic only of heathenism; it is

equally true of the Christian religion. Here in America, Christianity is embraced as a philosophy, but it is rejected as a way of life. We are happy to build churches, publish Bibles, and hire pastors, but we don't want to live by the code that Jesus taught. We boast of having more religious broadcasts in both radio and television than all other nations of the world put together, and it is reported that we employ a full-time Christian worker for every 250 Christians in our nation, but it is difficult to tell the difference between the lifestyles of American Christians and non-Christians. In concept, we Americans are Christians; in conduct, we are humanists. We are much like the rich young ruler who came to Jesus, asking to be made a disciple. He loved Christ's teachings, for he evaluated the price of discipleship as being far too great; so he left Christ's presence *"very sorrowful"* (see Luke 18:23).

Christianity is generally viewed by America's intellectual society as being neither practical nor powerful. It has been replaced by social and political action. As a result, our country is governed by the regulation of laws rather than by a relationship with the Lord. We look to the state rather than to the Scriptures, and the highest level of authority in our land is the Supreme Court rather than the Supreme Being. Christian America is now court-controlled, not conscience-guided. "In God we trust" fits our coins, but not our conduct, for government, investments, and insurance have just about replaced God as the source of our confidence.

Is this commonly accepted philosophy that the state is more practical than the Scriptures consistent with experience? Has the American democratic government made life more functional than the provisions God has made in His Word? Do not the unrest, the rising poverty level, the ever-enlarging national budget deficits, the increasing crime rate, and the recurring racial tensions bear strong evidence that man is far less benefitted by self-rule than he is by divine rule?

When God accepted the responsibility of bringing Israel out of Egypt into the promised land, He gave them laws and regulations that were functional in every area of human and divine relationships. The Ten Commandments provided practical moral principles which formed a working basis for people's relationship with God and with one another. No society has yet been able to improve on these extremely practical principles of behavior, and English law as we now know it, is based upon these premises.

The statutes and regulations that God gave to Moses on Mount Sinai were equally as practical for day-to-day living. They gave guidance in the handling and eating of food, in sanitation, in social relationships, in property management, in inheritances, in marriages, and in the use of human sexuality. God even provided for human government for His people.

Was all of this successful? It was completely so, as long as the people willingly obeyed the laws of God; but every time they thought they had a better idea, they found themselves in such dire trouble that they had to cry out to the Lord for deliverance. They could not add God's way to their way, nor was the addition of their concepts ever an improvement on God's provision. The history of Israel's rise and fall as a nation is divided into those periods of obedience and disobedience to God's regulations. Obedience equaled success, while disobedience always produced failure. Doing it God's way consistently proved to be practical, although it didn't always seem to be logical and was seldom very popular. Somehow the human spirit desires to rule rather than to be ruled.

God's guidelines for daily living are as practical for twentieth-century Christians as they were for Abraham, Moses, David, or Paul. Specific regulations have varied throughout the years, but the principles remain unchanged. Israel's food laws, for instance, were based as much upon availability, sanitation, and preservation as on anything else, and the New Testament establishes that it is the principle, not the precept, that believers are to observe, for God told Peter that anything that He has called clean should no longer be called unclean.

Has society developed better guidelines for marriage than the Bible provides? Our divorce rate is evidence to the contrary! Do we take better care of the poor than the Bible did with interest-free loans, the right of the poor to glean in the vineyards and fields during the harvest season, and the levying of a third tithe upon Israel to support her welfare system? Ask America's street people. Does our form of government surpass the rule of Moses, the leadership of Joshua, or the reign of David? Moses ruled Israel *with* God, while democracy increasingly seeks to rule *without* God. As God revealed to Daniel, and as history has attested, the further society gets from God-rule, the more degenerate it becomes, and the greater the decadence, the more consistently people depart from the principles of God. It is like the car released to roll downhill. The farther it goes, the faster it rolls, until it hits a stationary object that abruptly, and destructively, arrests its plunge. Civilization that departs from God always ends in self-destruction. The Psalmist put it this way: *"The wicked shall be turned into hell, and all the nations that forget God. For the needy shall not always be forgotten; the expectation of the poor shall not perish forever"* (Psalm 9:17-18).

What is true of political societies is equally true of the

body of believers we loosely call Christians. Peter declared that we are *"....a chosen generation, a royal priesthood, a holy nation, His own special people, that you may proclaim the praises of Him who called you out of darkness into His marvelous light"* (I Peter 2:9). In forming believers into *"a holy nation,"* God purposed that all other nations of the world could see a demonstration of the superiority of divine government over human government. God's desire is not enforcement, but enticement. At this time, He does not demand that nations bow to His government, but He does desire to demonstrate the superiority of that government by prospering His saints and His Church in all areas of life as He did in the days of David and Solomon. God loves to provoke to jealousy by greatly favoring those who willingly submit to His rule and authority.

This is not to suggest, however, that the Bible was written as a textbook for economics, social behavior, or political science. The Bible was written to reveal God and to make clear that there is a means of approach for each person into the presence of God. That means of approach is called a conversion, and it is such a dramatic and amazing experience that the Bible refers to it as being "born again." Paul wrote, *"Therefore, if anyone is in Christ, he is a new creation; old things have passed away; behold, all things have become new"* (2 Corinthians 5:17). The New Testament in Today's English puts it this way: *"When anyone is joined to Christ he is a new being; the old is gone, the new has come. All this is done by God, who through Christ changed us from enemies into his friends, and gave us the task of making others his friends also"* (verse 18 added).

Life begins anew at Calvary, or at least that is God's provision for us. Not only is sin forgiven, but the Adamic nature is replaced with a divine nature, worldly thought patterns are supplanted by spiritual thought patterns, and old habits are succeeded by new ones. The person who once walked in self-will is enabled to "walk in the Spirit," while he who once had only his own resources to rely upon now has access to all the resources of God.

Every New Testament reference to a Christian speaks of this vital change, for we are called "the family of God," "sons of God," "heirs of God," and even the "bride of Christ." All of this implies something far more radical than mere forgiveness of our sins; it involves being changed into something we never even dreamed about before.

For some persons this becomes a totally new way of life, while for others it is used as a means of escape from life. Many Christians want a relationship without responsibility and a conversion without change. Like the Philistines who added the ark of God to the house of their gods, some Christians seek to merely add God to their own way of life. They are sometimes referred to as "Sunday Christians," for that is the only day when they participate in anything that is classified as Christian. They live a "normal" life all week and then live "spiritually" on the Lord's day.

Such mixture was unacceptable in the early Church, and it is still unacceptable to God, for being a Christian is far more than an experience; it is a life received and lived. The heart of the gospel is not just that Christ died for us, but that Christ *lives* in us. John said, *"And this is the testimony: that God has given us eternal life, and this life is in His Son. He who has the Son has life; he who does not have the Son of God does not have life"* (I John 5:11-12). This life cannot be hidden as a candle under a bushel basket; it must be lived or it will atrophy. The Christian life cannot be put on deposit; it must be put on display.

After one is born again, it is live or die—not live a double life!

I am not saying that Christians are deceitful; I am observing that they are often selfish and confused over what the Christian life actually is. They have lived in servitude to the gods of this world so long that, like Israel, they tend to worship the Lord God of heaven with their lips and religious activities, but they serve the gods of commerce, pleasure, and humanism during the week. They have not yet learned to lose their lives for Christ's sake in order to truly find the life of Christ being lived within themselves. To them, being a Christian means going to church on Sundays, singing in the choir or teaching a Sunday school class, and wearing a church pin during the week. They will pay their tithes and praise their pastor, but once the Sunday service is over, they live very much like their neighbors live. It seems that no one has taught them that after being received into the family of God, they have been installed as ambassadors of heaven in their neighborhoods. They are expected to live like citizens of heaven and to be representatives of God everywhere they go. They have a practical responsibility to live, act, talk, walk, think, and relate as godly representatives to this world. There is never room for selfish behavior when we are on duty.

Ours is not the first generation to substitute religious behavior for spiritual living. Isaiah was a channel for God to remind Israel that her rituals, sacrifices, and fastings were far off target because they did not produce practical behavior in the day-to-day world. God cried through Isaiah, *"Is this not the fast that I have chosen: to loose the bonds of wickedness, to undo the heavy burdens, to let the oppressed go free, and that you break every yoke? Is it not to share your bread with the hungry, and that you bring to your house the poor who are cast out; when you see the naked, that you cover him, and not hide yourself from your own flesh?"* (Isaiah 58:6-7).

It is not enough that we have received the grace of God; we must share that grace with others. It is wonderful that we have entered into the gifts of the Spirit, but are we using them to alleviate human misery in and out of the Church? The compassion that has come to us should flow through us, and the provisions a gracious God has shared with us need to be shared with those who have not yet met this blessed Lord. *"Freely you have received, freely give"* (Matthew 10:8) is Christ's command. We are not Joseph's storehouse; we are Christ's river of living waters flowing out to a needy world. People should not have to come to buy from us; we should flow out freely to them.

No one likes the song, the shout, the dance, and the praise of the Lord any more than I do. I have written books about this, and I have traveled the world teaching it, but if all we have is the exuberant expression of our love for the Lord, we have seriously shortchanged ourselves. Christ brought us life that is as practical *to* us as it is *through* us. No one should have a better grasp on mental health than the Christian who has received the mind of Christ. It is the born again person who has solved the riddle of life—he knows who he is and what his purpose is in life. The complexities of marriage are more easily handled when the principles of God's Word are applied to the intimate relationships of the home, for the Bible deals with every aspect, from courtship through child-raising. Even the confusion of today's economics can be softened when we accept and adopt God's financial plan for our lives.

God is a very practical God, and His Book is as practical for human behavior as a manufacturer's instruction book.

The Bible was written to make life practical, not miserable. Happy is the Christian who daily reads the Bible, but practical is the person who lives what he reads in that Bible. It is not what we memorize, but what we personalize that makes God's Word become a practical guide to everyday living. It has well been said that "the best binding for the Bible is human skin."

It is quite common for people of the world to submit themselves to an analysis program that costs them thousands of dollars, and all they gain is some insight into their problems. Christians who have disciplined themselves to daily prayer have access to more than insight into their problems; they have the wisdom of God available to them to give them the solution to those problems, plus they have access to the power of God to help them implement that wisdom in effecting true changes in their lives. Furthermore, all of this is paid for by God Himself. Could anything be more practical than that?

The coarse fisherman who traveled with Jesus understood the practicality of the Christian life, for he wrote, *"... His divine power has given to us all things that pertain to life and godliness, through the knowledge of Him who called us by glory and virtue, by which have been given to us exceedingly great and precious promises, that through these you may be partakers of the divine nature, having escaped the corruption that is in the world through lust"* (2 Peter 1:3-4).

Practical Peter was convinced that God, through Christ, has already given to us everything that pertains to life and godliness. It is interesting that he put "life" before "godliness." Peter had learned through his experiential relationship with Jesus that there would never be any necessary thing lacking in his daily life if he was following Jesus at that moment. He had seen the water turned to wine, the loaves and fish multiplied, the sea calmed, and the fish obey Christ's command, and he had been a participant in miracles of healing. Peter believed that those who are partakers of the divine nature are also partakers in the divine supply. To his dying day, Peter never faced a situation in life that was beyond the ability and availability of Christ.

Peter saw beyond the positive practicality of possessions received because of the indwelling nature of Christ Jesus and looked into the protection of *"having escaped the corruption that is in the world through lust."* He could not equate the presence of the divine with the presence of the demonic; he was convinced that the indwelling of God's divine nature enabled us to escape the corruption of the present world system. This means that we are not subject to corruption: we are carriers of righteousness. We need not fear being affected or infected by the world; it is the world that is in danger of being infected by the divine life that dwells within us. *"Greater is He that is in you, than he that is in the world"* (I John 4:4), John assured us. We need not live defensively; our foe has been conquered at Calvary!

How, then, should we live in this present world? As lights shining in a dark place. As ambassadors of heaven on assignment. As possessors of eternity while still locked in this time/space capsule. Paul summarized it in his letter to Titus when he wrote, *"For the grace of God that brings salvation has appeared to all men, teaching us that, denying ungodliness and worldly lusts, we should live soberly, righteously, and godly in the present age, looking for the blessed hope and glorious appearing of our great God and Savior, Jesus Christ, who gave Himself for us, that He might redeem us from every lawless deed and purify for*

Himself His own special people, zealous for good works" (Titus 2:11-14).

We are, indeed, "God's own special people." We are indwelt with God's Spirit, and we have received eternal life. This is superiority beyond anything that the world has ever known, and this superiority should make us the most practical people in all of the world. Nothing on earth is more practical than the Christian life, if it is lived consistently, and nothing is more painful than trying to apply Christian principles to a carnal way of life. How desperately God desires His Church on earth to keep her head in heaven and her feet on the earth. He still wants all to mount up with wings as eagles, and to walk without fainting (see Isaiah 40:31).

God is neither a luxury nor a necessity to our life—He is our life! Dr. R.A. Torrey used to say it well: "He is Lord of all, or not Lord at all." God has redeemed us unto Himself so that, as the Body of Christ, we can be the agents for the revelation of God and His kingdom to this present age. How practical—and how gracious!

(From *Times of Refreshing*)

41

The Believer in the Church

A Church Was Born

Paul, the student of Gamaliel, proved his exceptional skill with words and spiritual concepts in what we know as the Pauline epistles of the New Testament. Whether he was dealing with concepts of God's redemption or conditions of relationship with God, Paul never seemed to lack for words to express both his viewpoint and his feelings. This inspired gift of communication seemed to fail him, however, when he wrote: *"Without controversy great is the mystery of godliness: God was manifest in the flesh, justified in the Spirit, seen of angels preached unto the Gentiles, believed on in the world, received up into glory"* (1 Timothy 3:16). It is a masterpiece of brevity, condensation, and understatement.

"Great is the mystery?" "Stupendous" might be a better word. The prophets, looking forward to the coming of the Messiah, could not comprehend how God would do it or the eternal ramifications of this coming, for theirs was a very limited and partial picture. Even the disciples who lived with this God-man did not understand the depths of

43

the revelation that God was making through His Son, and Paul, looking backward to Christ's coming, could say little more than "great is the mystery."

The Perplexity of Christmas

Mary, the mother of Jesus, who very likely was but a teenage girl at the time, could not grasp the monumental event in which she was to play a key role. She willingly offered her body for God's service, but even angelic communication could not illuminate her mind to apprehend what was actually about to happen. God was about to become flesh with us. Eternal God was about to become a space-time limited man.

Can we, in this enlightened twentieth century, understand this action of God any better than they did? Do we comprehend how the omnipresent God would limit Himself to a body that would never travel more than fifty miles in any direction? Can we grasp what it meant for the omnipotent God to subject Himself to the oppression of the Roman conquerors?

At best we can but join Paul in admitting, "Great is the mystery." Enormous is the enigma of God made flesh; prodigious is the problem of the God-man preaching to the Gentiles; mammoth is the mystery of God becoming sinful flesh in order to redeem us back to saintly status. Christmas, at its best, is a colossal conundrum to the contemplative Christian. We cannot understand it, but we can accept, believe, and benefit from it. Like Paul, we can but say, *"The life which I now live in the flesh I live by the faith of the Son of God, who loved me, and gave himself for me"* (Galatians 2:20).

The Philosophy of Christmas

The philosophy of Christmas does not begin in the first

chapter of Matthew, but in the first chapter of Genesis. God created the heavens, the earth, and mankind for His own pleasure, for John heard the twenty-four elders in heaven say to God, *"Thou hast created all things, and for thy pleasure they are and were created"* (Rev. 4:11). Man, the highest of God's creation, was made in the image and likeness of God which made it possible for God to have affectionate fellowship with this creation. The walks and the talks in the Garden of Eden in the cool of the evening are well documented in the Scriptures, as is the fact that this was fulfilling and completing to God. God even took a companion out of Adam's side and made him one who would complete him very similar to the way Adam was taken out of God to complete God's need for a love object. But this union and communion was disrupted by disobedience, and Adam and Eve were driven from the garden and their companionship with God. Sin separated what creation had united, and God was left without a man with whom to have fellowship.

The Pursuit for Companionship

Many hundreds of years later God gained in Enoch what He had lost in Adam, but when Enoch was translated, as likely was God's original plan for Adam, God again found Himself without a man on the earth with whom to have fellowship. Then God revealed Himself to Noah, and for several hundred years He and Noah had fellowship based on relationship, but Noah died. By the time God could get the attention of another man on this earth, the world had been completely repopulated after the flood, and civilization was quite highly developed, especially in the field of the arts and sciences. Abram, a resident of Ur in the Chaldean civilization, finally heard God's voice and responded obediently. At this point, God

45

determined to bring forth a nation who would respond to Him so that there could be continuity in His relationship with mankind. Slowly this nation was formed, and then God sent them into Egypt for training. Four hundred years later He led this people out of their bondage, back toward their homeland, under the guidance of Moses.

Through a series of miraculous events, God brought the Israelites to Mount Sinai, and there He began to communicate with them directly from the cloud of smoke that covered the mountain. This whole experience terrified the people, and they sent their representatives to Moses with a message to go and tell God to never do this again. If God wanted anything done, He could just write it down, and they would do it. After all, they had been professional slaves for hundreds of years, hadn't they? They traded a proffer of relationship for the prohibitions of law, and God again found Himself both without fellowship with man and without a meaningful revelation of Himself to man.

The Projection of Companionship

In the ensuing years of God's dealing with this nation, He sent them prophets with both communication from and revelation of Himself, but the people could not see God in the prophets, and often so rejected God's message through them that they ultimately rejected and stoned the messengers. God so wanted to reveal Himself as a tender, loving, compassionate companion to mankind, but whether He spoke directly from the mountain, appeared in angelic form, or communicated through a prophet, people were terrified of God and expected to die if they had any contact with Him. Fearing to fellowship with God, men fled from God.

In His foreknowledge, God had prepared to meet this

fearful reluctance of men to relate to Himself and had purposed to actually become a man in order for men to be able to relate to God. In the prologue to his gospel, John declared, *"And the Word was made flesh, and dwelt among us, and we beheld his glory, the glory as of the only begotten of the Father, full of grace and truth"* (John 1:14). Success! When God was flesh, men could relate to Him, behold His glory, and see the Father in the Son. It is the only revelation of God throughout the Scriptures that has worked consistently.

Participation in Companionship

Many years later, John the youth wrote an epistle as John the aged, and he began that epistle by saying, *"That which was from the beginning, which we have heard, which we have seen with our eyes, which we have looked upon, and our hands have handled, of the Word of life;... that which we have seen and heard declare we unto you, that ye also may have fellowship with us: and truly our fellowship is with the Father, and with his Son Jesus Christ"* (1 John 1:1,3).

It really had worked! Men saw God in Jesus, and men were willing to fellowship with the Father through the Son. What sin had stolen in the garden, the incarnation restored at Bethlehem of Judea. God and men were united in fellowship again. It had merely required God to take on a body for men to return to fellowship with Him.

Take on "a" body? No, that's not quite accurate. Actually, God has needed three bodies in order to continuously reveal Himself to men and to have uninterrupted fellowship with us. At Bethlehem, through Mary's womb, God provided Himself a body that could die, for until sin was extirpated there could be no fellowship between a holy God and His sinful creatures. Since neither

47

God nor angels can die, it became necessary for God to become a man in order to absorb the death penalty that hung over mankind. The body worked perfectly, became our vicarious sacrifice, and died gloriously. As the Scriptures put it, *"Christ hath redeemed us from the curse of the law, being made a curse for us; for it is written, Cursed is every one that hangeth on a tree"* (Gal. 3:13). Body number one was formed, indwelt, utilized, and laid aside in the perfect will of God.

Body number two came forth from the tomb on that first Easter morning. The Bible declares, *"But now Christ is risen from the dead, and has become the firstfruits of those who have fallen asleep"* (1 Cor. 15:20). Jesus Christ, the God-man, not only blazed the trail through *"the valley of the shadow of death"* (Psalm 23:4), He also pioneered the path through the Resurrection, being the first to come from the dead in a glorified body.

In speaking of this resurrection from the dead, Paul wrote: *"The body is sown in corruption, it is raised in incorruption. It is sown in dishonor, it is raised in glory. It is sown in weakness, it is raised in power. It is sown a natural body, it is raised a spiritual body. There is a natural body, and there is a spiritual body"* (1 Cor. 15:42-44). Christ came out of the tomb in a very different form than He went into it. This second body is now seated at the right hand of the Father interceding on our behalf as our faithful High Priest (*see* Hebrews 10:12-24).

Perpetuation of Companionship

As necessary and needful as this glorified body is to the program of God, the Ascension of Christ Jesus left the world without a visible demonstration of God to which men could comfortably relate, or at least it appeared to create such a void. But God had already prepared a third body for Himself through which He could manifest His person, presence, and power to mankind. The first body was called **JESUS**—*"Thou shalt call his name JESUS: for he shall save his people from their sins"* (Matt. 1:21). The second body was called **CHRIST**—*"For Christ has...entered...into heaven itself, now to appear in the presence of God for us"* (Heb. 9:24), and the third body is called the **CHURCH**—*"He is the head of the body, the church"* (Col. 1:18). The manifestation of God that was so successful through Jesus now continues through His many membered body which is the Church.

The Church is God's Ministry on Earth

Before the birth of Christ, the earth had been without divine ministry for several hundred years. There had been no anointed prophet or priest, and the religious system was long on tradition and liturgy, but short on truth and life. Jesus was a shock to the religious community of His day because He ministered in spiritual authority with divine energy and power.

God has purposed that the world should never again have to go without spiritual authority and ministry. In His High Priestly prayer, Jesus told the Father, *"As You sent Me into the world, I also have sent them into the world"* (John 17:18), and after His resurrection, Jesus told the disciples directly, *"As the Father has sent me, I also send you"* (John 20:21). The many-membered man which forms the body of the Church, is commissioned to continue the ministry of Jesus throughout time. Jesus promised, *"He that believeth on me, the works that I do shall he do also; and greater works than these shall he do; because I go unto my Father"* (John 14:12).

This world cannot know divine compassion if it does not feel it in the Church. The lost cannot know the love of

49

God unless the Church extends that love to them. The transforming power of God remains an unknown quotient unless the Church both demonstrates and offers it in every generation. Pleading for God to minister to our sick world seems out of order. The Church should perform that ministry in the name of Jesus. Why do we cry for God to do what we have been commissioned to do? As the Body of Christ, we are His extended hands of service and ministry; we are His heart of love and compassion. God's ministry comes through His body, the Church.

The Church is God's Government on Earth

Christ Jesus, in His glorified body, is now seated in the heavens as our High Priest, and into His hands has been committed all dominion, authority, and power. For it has been decreed, *"that at the name of Jesus, every knee should bow of things in heaven, and things in the earth, and things under the earth; and that every tongue should confess that Jesus Christ is Lord, to the glory of God the Father"* (Phil. 2:10-11).

It is "at the name of Jesus" that divine government is exercised, and that name has been shared with the Church on earth. We have been given this name through the new birth, by marriage, and by power of attorney. Subsequent to being born again, *"the Spirit himself bears witness with our spirit that we are the children of God, and if children, then heirs; heirs of God, and joint heirs with Christ"* (Romans 8:16-17). This sonship with God and heirship with Jesus gives us the divine family name, with all of its rank, authority, and privileges. Having declared this bearing of the divine name, Paul adds, *"For the earnest expectation of the creation eagerly waits for the revealing of the sons of God... because the creation itself also will be delivered from the bondage of corruption into the glorious liberty of the children of God"* (Rom. 8:19,21). Creation recognizes the authority and government of God in the Church on earth, and so does the demonic.

We have not only been born to the name, we have been married into that name, for the Church is also called "the bride of Christ." The key factor in a marriage ceremony is the conferring of the man's name to the woman. Weddings traditionally end with, "May I present to you Mr. and Mrs. (whatever the man's last name may be)." In marriage the woman relinquishes her family name to accept the husband's family name, and from that day forward she transacts all business in her husband's name. So does the Church! We have been instructed, *"Whatsoever ye do in word or deed, do all in the name of the Lord Jesus"* (Col. 3:17).

The Church, as Christ's body on earth, and bearing His name on earth, becomes God's government on earth. *"Now then we are ambassadors for Christ, as though God did beseech you by us..."* (2 Cor. 5:20), Paul wrote. Heaven is our citizenship, earth is our embassy, government is our responsibility, and representation is our mission. This earth only knows divine government as she sees it in God's Church.

The Church is God's Glory on the Earth

Paul concludes his delightful doxology by saying that glory to God comes through the Church. He wrote, *"Now to Him who is able to do exceedingly abundantly above all that we ask or think, according to the power that works in us, to Him be glory in the church by Christ Jesus throughout all ages, world without end. Amen"* (Ephesians 3:20-21). Furthermore, in His High Priestly prayer to the Father, Jesus said, *"The glory which thou gavest me I have given them"* (John 17:22), and the

51

doctrinal book of Romans declares, *"Moreover whom He predestined, these He also called; whom He called, these He also justified; and whom He justified, these He also glorified"* (Romans 8:30). The glory of God that was resident in Jesus is now resident in the Church. If the world is ever to know the glory of God it must be displayed and demonstrated in the Church here on earth. God's glory is not ethereal, it is spiritual, and we are the spiritual body of Christ here on the earth.

The Church is God on earth

If Jesus was God made flesh on this earth, and if the Church is the body of Christ on this earth (Colossians 1:24 clearly declares that we are), then the Church is the earthly manifestation of God. Jesus is in heaven—warmly associated with the portion of the Church that has already entered heaven by the route of death. In this position, He is declared to be *"the head of the church: and he is the savior of the body. Therefore...the church is subject unto Christ..."* (Eph. 5:22-23). The vital relationship between the head and the body is obvious. Christ, the head of the body, conceives and commands, while the Church, the body, responds to and executes those commands. The initiative is His; the implementation is ours. He is in heaven; we are on earth, but we function as one!

Paul was so convinced by the Spirit that we Christians form the body of Christ here on the earth, that he wrote of it several times. He spoke of us being individual members of the body, and then wrote, *"We are members of his body, of his flesh, and of his bones"* (Eph. 5:30). Could anything be more imperative or more intimate? Just as our children are formed of our substance, so the Church is formed of the substance of God. We not only have His name, we also have His nature. Therefore God dares to set us up as His personal representative here on earth. God appears on earth in His Church. We more than represent God—we reveal God, for Christ is in us, and this is the only hope of glory here on the earth (see Col. 1:27). What a confusing characterization of God our segmented, factional Church must be presenting to the world, but, immature as we are, the Church is the only representation of God on the face of the earth.

The Birth of This Church

The Church was not born quickly. Its delivery was slow and deliberate. As incomprehensible as it may seem that God was made flesh to become the Savior of the world, more was born that day in Bethlehem of Judea than a mere Deliverer. The birth of Christ was also the beginning of the birth of the Church that was to have world-wide ramifications and eternal authority and activity. Repeatedly Christ is called *"the head of the Church"* (see Eph. 5:23 and Col. 1:18), and in a normal birth the head of the child comes first. The Church did not experience a breech birth; it came head first.

The body of the Church did not appear until Calvary, when the Roman spear pierced the side of Jesus Christ, and what had been a substance closest to His heart poured forth to the earth. Just as God had taken a portion of the side of Adam ("rib" in *King James Version*) and formed it into His bride, Eve, so God took the substance from the side of Jesus and formed it into the Church which is to become Christ's bride. We are not adopted, in the sense of mere legal placement, we are created in the image of Christ Jesus; made of the very substance of God. The Church, quite literally, came out of the body of Christ Jesus. She has been formed of His substance much as Adam was formed of the substance of God.

53

This child, the Church, was beautiful but still dependent upon the umbilical life-supply of Jesus until the Day of Pentecost when the breath of God became the breath of the Church. The mighty rushing wind that accompanied the coming of God's Spirit became the breath of life for the Church, and in the energy of that divine Spirit the Church has continued to live and function to this very day. Where this breath of God is restricted, resisted, or rejected, the Church lives in a spiritual oxygen tent, or it dies.

The Purpose of Christmas

How we miss the heart of God's purposes if we can see in Christmas nothing more than the coming of One Who would save us from sin. That is a valid view, but it is a restricted view. Salvation from sin is but part of a birth process intended to reproduce God on the earth in the form of the Church. Our salvation somewhat equates to gestation, for when we are saved, we are placed in Christ; later these "saved ones" come from His side as living members of His Church on earth.

Christmas was Immanuel—"God with us"—and the Church on earth has become God's "Emmanuel" to mankind. Born in Christ, brought from His side, and endued by His Spirit, we are His body on earth and shall be His bride in heaven. Little wonder that Paul had to exclaim, *"This is a great mystery: but I speak concerning Christ and the church"* (Eph. 5:33). I feel that way every Christmas.

(From *Times of Refreshing*)

The Church in the World

That the next move of God is going to come to and through local congregations seems to be widely held by many nationally known preachers. The Spirit is quickening our hearts to realize that Christ did not die for Christian publications, Christian television, or Christian conventions; He loved and died for His Church. Parachurch activities and interchurch ministries may well minister to the Body of Christ as a supplement, but they can never succeed as a substitute for a local congregation.

To the Church, which God calls "glorious," He mercifully gave His Son, His Spirit, and then apostles, prophets, evangelists, pastors, and teachers. There are those who declare that these gifts have been given to the Body of Christ "at large," but the New Testament seems to indicate that they have been given to the local congregations, who then comprise the Body "at large."

The Church is INCOMPATIBLE with the World

Anyone who looks beyond the organizational structure of a local church must admit that God's Church on earth is incompatible with the world system. In trying to apply this fact to the daily lives of members of the Church, some leaders have delighted in quoting, *"Come out from among them and be separate, says the Lord. Do not touch what is unclean, and I will receive you. I will be a Father to you, and you shall be My sons and daughters, says the Lord Almighty"* (2 Corinthians 6:17-18). Their application of this verse tends to breed asceticism, sectarianism, and an uninvolvement with life.

This is vastly different from Christ's prayer to the Father when He prayed, *"I have given them Your word; and the world has hated them because they are not of the world, just as I am not of the world. I do not pray that You should take them out of the world, but that You should keep them from the evil one"* (John 17:14-15). The Church is *in* the world but not *of* the world. We have been called to separation from worldliness, not from the world. Christ's letters to the seven churches of Asia censored them for allowing the world system to infiltrate them, but He did not condemn them for being in the midst of the world— that was where they were needed.

The Church is INVISIBLE to the World

The man of the world is no more aware of Christ's Church than a dog is aware of the writings of Mark Twain. To him, the Church is invisible at all times; the Church is mystical. Unfortunately, this same attitude prevails in the minds of many Christians. They so emphasize the mystical, invisible Church that they fail to realize that God has designated the Church to reveal Christ to the world. Just as Jesus revealed the Father, congregations reveal the Church. God is seen only pragmatically in nature, but He can be seen personally in the Church.

For many years, I was taught that I had been "saved to serve," but as I have matured spiritually, I am far more convinced that I have been redeemed to reveal the Father. Unless the Church functions in a God-like fashion, God will not be seen on this earth. Our motives, manners, methods, and even the way we handle our money must be consistent with God's nature.

The Church is INDISPENSABLE in the World

When our emphasis ceases to be exclusively celestial and begins to include the terrestrial, the world will begin to see the "invisible" Church as an active part of earth's society. As the local church rises up to become active in politics, social affairs, morality, and the economy, the world tends to see us as a meddlesome minority that must be either continenced or countered, and historically the governments of the world have preferred to persecute or ignore the Church.

What they obviously do not realize is that the Church is *indispensable* in the world. The Church is the salt of the earth, both flavoring and preserving society. Even persons who despise the local church will refuse to purchase a home in a community that has no church. Furthermore, the Church is the light of the world. The darkness of the Middle Ages might well prevail into the present if it were not for the Church of Jesus Christ on this earth. We have repeatedly been shown that major scientific breakthroughs and inventions have come through enlightened Christians. The Church is God's major witness on this earth, and God has purposed that the Church be His enforcement agency for implementing divine government here and now.

If the world system could effectively destroy the Church on earth, the world would soon find itself without truth, compassion, tenderness, love, law, righteousness, or hope, for these are all by-products of the gospel that have no parallel in the kingdom of Satan. On a day-by-day basis, Christ's Church on earth flows these spiritual ingredients into the mainstream of society. Just as the human body is lifeless without the flow of a bloodstream, so society is lifeless without the flow of the Church and what she offers this present world.

The Church is INVINCIBLE in the World

Jesus taught us that there would be constant conflict between the world and the true Church. He said that we would be hated for our righteousness and because we represent another world. This hatred is more than philosophical; it has been manifested very physically. Multiple thousands of people have been tortured and martyred for their testimony in our generation. Satan has no love for God's kingdom or for God's kids!

There have been times when it appeared that Satan's kingdom would in over the Church, but those were only battles lost; the war has been won by Christ in the midst of His Church! Hallelujah! Jesus told us, *"These things I have spoken to you, that in Me you may have peace. In the world you will have tribulation; but be of good cheer, I have overcome the world"* (John 16:33). "We can't lose for winning."

Following Peter's confession of faith, Jesus said, *"On this rock I will build My church, and the gates of Hades shall not prevail against it"* (Matthew 16:18). In ancient days, the gates of the city were the ordinary place for transacting business, administering justice, and conducting trials. They were the city halls and county courthouses of their day. When Jesus said that *"the gates of Hades shall not prevail,"* He was dealing with an enemy that has tried unsuccessfully to destroy the Church of the Lord Jesus Christ here upon this earth. Satan's strategy has been to turn his hostility toward the Christian and to attack him and the earthly Church he represents.

His favorite method has been to use satanic councils

against the Church. He uses opinion, the courts, philosophy, education, and even religion to hinder the work of God's Church and to discredit its members. But Jesus said that this ungodly council would not prevail against the Church on earth.

Kenneth Wuest victoriously translates this passage, *"The councils of the unseen world shall not overpower the church."* Adam Clarke adds a triumphant note in saying, "Though hell should open her gates and the devil and all his angels fight against Christ and His followers, the arm of omnipotence shall prevail. Neither the plots, strategies nor strength of Satan or his angels will ever prevail." Hallelujah!

The gates of death are a citadel, but the Church of Jesus is a stronghold built on a firm foundation. The council of the ungodly will not prevail against the council of the Church, *unless* the Church either submits to the world's "wisdom" or refuses to follow the divine wisdom given to us in Christ Jesus. The Church is invincible as long as she is unquestionably following her leader and indelibly stamping God's image on the world in which she lives.

World, watch out! Ready or not, here comes Christ's Church convinced that divine principles in Christ's Church are incompatible with the world. We may seem small enough to be invisible to many, but we are persuaded that we are indispensable to society in the world. Furthermore, we know that in Christ Jesus, the Church mystical and the Church visible is invincible in the world. Righteousness shall prevail, and we intend to be a consistent demonstration of that righteousness.

(From *Harvest Time*)

My People Shall Never Be Ashamed

The minor prophet Joel is best known as the source for Peter's quote on the day of Pentecost, saying, *"This is that which was spoken by the prophet Joel... '*[God said] *"I will pour out of my Spirit upon all flesh..."* '(Acts 2:16-17). This minor prophet graphically describes the ruin of the Church in the first chapter of his book, but he gloriously delineates the restoration of the Church in chapter two. Twice in this chapter, Joel declares that God said, *"My people shall never be ashamed"* (verses 26-27).

If this statement is taken out of context, the verses are untrue, for there is much for which today's Church to be ashamed of. Surely, we should be ashamed of the wholesale turning from the Word of the Lord in many Christian circles today, and we cannot help being ashamed of the apparent sinfulness among God's people, even among some of our leadership. Are we not ashamed of the terrible lacking of spiritual waters in most churches, and of the powerlessness of many of God's people? Even when introspectively searching our own hearts, are we not ashamed that we have done so little with the great abundance Christ has imparted to us?

Sound exegesis never allows the separation of a text from its context, and it dare not be allowed with this second chapter of Joel, for this promise of unashamedness cannot be separated from the context and still remain valid. Following the promise that *"the Lord will do great things"* (verse 21), we are urged to *"be glad then, ye children of Zion, and rejoice in the Lord your God"* (verse 23) because God did send the rain, and He sent it in its proper season. The former rain came, making it possible for the plowman to break the soil, and He sent the latter rain so that the seed could sprout and bring forth new life.

Is not the water supply of the Spirit available to the Church at the Church's command rather than at the caprice of God or some undefined cycle of the moving of God? Is it a sovereign act of God that one church seems to have an abundant supply of the Spirit while another is dry and parched, or is it that the first church did what was necessary to have the rain, while the second merely tried to get along with what they had? God has provided the rain. There is always an ample supply of the Holy Spirit's ministry.

If the rain is totally dependent upon God's sovereign action, it will be difficult to enter into rejoicing even in the midst of the rain, for there will be a fear that it won't last long, and drought will certainly follow it. Those who have lived in the farm belt will attest that farmers generally fear and expect the worst, even to the point of being unable to enjoy profitable weather seasons. There is always the fear that it won't be enough; it will never be repeated, or that it will be followed by some disaster.

Many Christian believers react similarly. They never expect a moving of God's presence to last—but why not? God does not begin a work He is unable or unwilling to complete. Any work of God that fails to come to completion has been hindered by man, not abandoned by

God. We can rejoice when the rains come, knowing that when rain is needed at a later season, it too will come from the heavens. As our worship ascends, God's rain of the Spirit descends.

"He which hath begun a good work in you will perform it until the day of Jesus Christ" (Philippians 1:6), Paul declared. Our response to the movings of God should never be dread or fear that it will not last—it will last if we want it to last. It will last if we will live in it as God gives it to us.

As the result of God's pouring out of His Spirit on a continuing basis, three things will happen. First, *"the floors shall be full of wheat"* (verse 24). In the New Testament, the wheat, or grain, is often spoken of as the Word of God. It is this that the sower went forth in anticipation of the harvest. The pledge is that there will be an ample abundance of the Word—the floors will be absolutely full with heaping piles of wheat of the Word. This is the first thing that the outpouring of the Holy Spirit produces: a harvest of the Word of God. This is not equated to a harvest of souls; it is a harvest of the Word. An abundance of the Word will bring a harvest of souls, but God's Spirit brings a proliferation of the Word. We can never bring forth the living Word without the Spirit, but where the Spirit reigns supreme, the floors will be filled with the Word.

There is no reason for any church to have a famine of the Word of God. Oh, I know Amos tells us of such a famine, and I can illustrate it from what I have observed in my travels. It's happening far too rapidly in America, but there is no reason for it except our own neglect. Sometimes we have eaten all the wheat God gave us, and we had a marvelous meal, but we did not save any of it for sowing. The New Testament teaches us that some of the grain is

63

for planting, and some of it is for bread (see 2 Corinthians 9:10). Any farmer who eats an entire harvest will be unable to plant his fields the following season, and any church who consumes everything God gives without reserving seed for a subsequent harvest will have to live in memory and misery.

The second result of the outpouring of God's Spirit is that *"the vats shall overflow with wine..."* (verse 24). Quite consistently throughout the Scriptures, wine speaks of joy—the highest elixir of joy that man has been able to produce. Peter said, to those who criticized the saints who had just been filled with the Spirit on the day of Pentecost, *"...these are not drunken, as ye suppose..."* (Acts 2:15); they had another source for their joy. It was the joyful, unrestrained, non-repressed responses that caused people to think that they were drunk. It is not too amazing that the Scripture frequently uses the word "wine" as a symbol for unrepressed joy, elation, and jubilation, for when the floors are covered with wheat, and faith says rain will come when it is needed, joy wells up within the people. Harvest season has traditionally been a time for festivity.

The third result of this outpouring of the Holy Spirit is that *"...the vats shall overflow with...oil"* (verse 24), and we know that "oil" is a consistent type of the Holy Spirit in the Bible. There will not only come the rain of the Spirit to help the Word produce; there will be the joy of the Spirit and the oil of the Spirit for fire, illumination, lubrication, medication, and for so many other blessings.

We do not possess a limited quantity of this oil. *"The vats overflow"*—it is in storage. The New Testament teaches that the Spirit is within us. We are not limited to outside forces graciously and beneficently raining the goodness of the Spirit upon us; we have stored within us the overflowing vats of the oil of the Spirit. He came to be resident within us. Hallelujah!

In the light of the fact that we have all of the wheat we can eat, all of the wine we can handle, and all of the oil we can use, God says, through Joel, *"I will restore to you..."* (verse 25), and then He lists four separate enemies of the vine that have ravished the church in times past. The *locust* is the destroyer of fruit; the *cankerworm* eats the bark, and the *palmerworm* eats the roots. This is about the order of destruction that God ordains through His "great army" which He sends among His disobedient people. First the fruit is destroyed, and if there is no repentance, He will work down the leaves, stem, and finally attack the very roots. Happy is the person who surrenders to the Lord at the fist stroke of judgment; he will not lose life, only fruit. If the leaves and bark remain untouched, the fruit can be regrown at another season, but if the roots are ruined, the plant is good only for burning.

All of this destruction was done by *"my great army which I sent among you"* (verse 25). God who builds up can tear down; He who gives can take away. We may prostitute God's love, but we will not long be allowed to prostitute His gifts; He will send in His little army to eat it up so that the fruit is not used in the kingdom of the devil.

Far too consistently, groups who have enjoyed beautiful moves of God turn away from relationship with God only to lose all life and maintain nothing but their former structure. They lose their fruit, leaves, bark, and even their roots, only to remain a stick in the ground, completely lifeless and worthless.

The promise of verse twenty-five is, *"I will restore to you the years the locust hath eaten..."* Those who have forsaken the ways of the living God, but return to Him after judgment, are promised such a bountiful harvest as

65

to restore to them the years of fruitlessness. What mercy! What grace! That is the way of the Lord. He takes from us only to train and correct us, and when He finally has us where He wants us, He restores bountifully, for He declares that *"it is more blessed to give than to receive"* (Acts 20:35). When the Church comes God's way, and gets back into divine order, God begins a restoring process whereby He no longer adds to the church; He multiplies. The fruitfulness lost during the season of departure is made up during the season of God's multiplication of harvest.

The final thrust of the context is, *"Ye shall eat in plenty, and be satisfied, and praise the name of the Lord your God, that hath dealt wondrously with you: and my people shall never be ashamed"* (verse 26). Those who are willing partakers of the great abundance of God's provision will never be ashamed. It is not enough to be surrounded by the Word, or even to be a student of the Word; we must be a *partaker* of the Word to never be ashamed. The key is not merely to know, but to eat. While the fad of America may be to diet, the goal of God is that we eat.

Not only will the partakers of the Word be unashamed, but those who have learned to "be satisfied" will never be ashamed. May God deliver us from the pernicious lusting after the new. It has damned many good churches, for a demand for the new opens the door for error, overemphasis of lesser truths, and an embracing of marginal doctrines. "What's new?" is too frequently a Christian greeting. How we need to accept that there is nothing new with God, and if we are moving in God, we will probably lack an awareness of anything being new; it will merely be renewed to us. Everything that God intended to reveal about Himself is contained in the Sacred Book. We dare not look for anything beyond its pages, but we can expect these truths to be renewed, made new, refreshed, living and vital to our hearts and lives. We don't have to have a new doctrine. It is not the new that is needed; it's the living! God give to us, out of His restoration, a willingness to be satisfied with His provision, for then we will never be ashamed.

Any church that has learned to eat plenty and be satisfied with God's provision will "praise the name of the Lord." Praise is inner health made audible, and unless we have it, we cannot display it, but when we have it, we cannot keep from showing it. Praise is less a learned response and more an automatic release. Praising people have no occasion to be ashamed.

Could any church that has known God's restoration, who has learned to eat in plenty and be satisfied and has entered into sufficient relationship with God to praise Him—could any such church be ashamed of God? Of course not! It is love, not shame, that we feel for God when the floors and vats are filled.

"My people shall never be ashamed." The only way to live in unashamedness is to live in the constancy of the presence of Christ. Paul declared, *"Behold, I lay in Zion a stumblingstone and rock of offence: and whosoever believeth on him shall never be ashamed" (Romans 9:33),* and *"Nevertheless I am not ashamed; for I know whom I have believed, and am persuaded that he is able to keep that which I have committed unto him against that day"* (2 Timothy 1:12). Out of relationship comes an awareness that we need not be ashamed: of God, of one another, of ourselves, or of our work for God.

John encouraged the early believers, *"And now, little children, abide in him; that, when he shall appear, we may have confidence, and not be ashamed before him at his*

67

coming" (1 John 2:28). Out of this relationship that brings restoration can come a walk before God that has no shame in it.

(From *Times of Refreshing*)

The Joy of the Kingdom

From the creation of Adam, God has never been without a kingdom on this earth. Sometimes His domain has seemed to be small, and other times it is revealed to be world-wide. God's dominion was first over one man, then a family, a clan, a race, and a nation. To say that God's kingdom has progressively increased is to view the kingdom totally from the human perspective. *"The earth is the LORD'S and all its fullness, The world and those who dwell therein,"* David sang (Psalm 24:1). God has always reigned in heaven and on earth, but humanity has been given the option to submit to that reign and enjoy the benefits of God's kingdom, or to resist God's rule and live outside the covenants of God.

The history of Israel is a divine demonstration of the value of accepting the theocratic dominion of God in personal and governmental affairs. These who had known the oppression of slavery for 400 years were released from bondage and progressively led to the land God had given to their forefather, Abraham. God became their Deliverer, their Protector, their Source of supply, their Law-giver, and their Guide. Jehovah loved them, led them, fed them, and fought their battles for them.

69

In return, God asked only for obedience and worship. Israel was not commissioned to form a kingdom for God; she was presented with that kingdom and asked to conform to it. The government that controlled their lives was not the result of committee action, but of divine revelation. The people did not enact the laws; they merely implemented them. It was obviously the kingdom of God, for its origin, its organization, and its method of operation were divine in nature.

Whenever the people of God's choice voluntarily submit to God's purposes and acknowledge Jehovah as their potentate, we have a manifestation of the kingdom of God on this earth. God's kingdom is neither limited to any one race of people nor does it exclude anyone. The kingdom is world-wide, culturally integrated, and eternal. No action of earthly politicians can erase it. Neither can ecclesiastical fiat alter it. It is the kingdom of God, and none can override it. Our only option is to ignore it, but that is about as effective as ignoring an approaching locomotive. Man in his frailty can stop neither of them.

Because this kingdom is divine in nature and spiritual in character, it is almost totally unknown to the average politician in our world. Since the kingdom of God has neither geographic boundaries nor political recognition, it has no seat in the United Nations Assembly. Its voice is never sought in the settlement of world disputes, and even the fragile demonstrations of that kingdom through the religious systems of the world are more tolerated than acknowledged. This is not as much a rejection as it is obvious ignorance, for God's true kingdom is known only to those who truly know God. Paul wrote, *"... in the wisdom of God, the world through wisdom did not know God"* (1 Corinthians 1:21).

In his letter to the believers in Rome, Paul the apostle

wrote, *"The kingdom of God is not eating and drinking, but righteousness and peace and joy in the Holy Spirit"* (Romans 14:17). This simple definition proves to be profound in its description, for it shifts the kingdom of God out of natural into the spiritual. It ignores the materialistic pursuit of possessions and inspires the inner recesses of the citizen. It shows us that God's kingdom is concerned with behavior and character rather than with belief and conduct. Reduced to its prime, God's kingdom is righteousness, peace, and **joy.** Everything else is periferal.

Joy is a Prospect of God's Kingdom

The very statement that God's kingdom is one of **joy** takes the kingdom out of the political arena of conflict, competition, and control which crush the souls of men and women and elevates it to a dominion of righteousness and peace which induce both the attitude and operation of joy.

That God's kingdom is inherently joyful is generously promised in the Bible. In looking at the King of this realm, David wrote, *"In Your presence is fullness of joy; at Your right hand are pleasures forevermore"* (Psalm 16:11), and when Isaiah looked at the nation, he wrote, *"You have multiplied the nation and increased its joy; they rejoice before You according to the joy of harvest, as men rejoice when they divide the spoil"* (Isaiah 9:3). In speaking of the citizens, he said, *"Instead of confusion they shall rejoice in their portion. Therefore in their land they shall possess double; everlasting joy shall be theirs"* (Isaiah 61:7).

Again and again, through prophet after prophet, God declared that His kingdom would be inhabited by joyful peoples. He said, "It shall be heard in this place... 'the voice of joy and the voice of gladness, the voice of the

71

bridegroom and the voice of the bride, the voice of those who will say: *"Praise the LORD of hosts, For the LORD is good, For His mercy endures forever"—and of those who will " 'bring the sacrifice of praise into the house of the LORD' "*(Jeremiah 33:10,11). Jehovah has promised, on the honor of His name, that **joy** would make up at least one third of His kingdom. Any politician could get elected on that platform, if he could convince people of his ability to fulfill that promise.

Joy is a Product of God's kingdom

Promises that have no substance to back them up are but empty lies that tend to make people prisoners of hope. God, Who cannot lie, has not merely promised **joy** in His kingdom; joy is actually a product of His kingdom. That kingdom is a kingdom of "righteousness," and where persons live in right relationship with one another, joy flows as naturally as water flows downhill. Most of the pain in our world is because of man's inhumanity to man. Broken relationships and greed for power and control over others have made life miserable rather than joyful for millions of persons, but God has provided a way for broken relationships to be restored. At Calvary, sin was dealt with conclusively. Its power has been broken, its penalty has been paid, and its very presence has been removed from the lives of believers. In its place is the righteousness of God which has been made available to us through Jesus Christ our Lord.

In God's kingdom, He deals far less with manifestation than with motivation. His grace has come to change our desires so that our performance will be righteous. We have not been given a new set of laws to observe so much as we have been given renewed hearts and minds that desire to do the will of God. Like David, we can say, *"I delight to do Your will, O my God"* (Psalm 40:8), and such an inner drive will maintain a high level of the righteousness of God both in our relationship with Himself and with others.

The wise man said, *"He who follows righteousness and mercy finds life, righteousness and honor"* (Proverbs 21:21). Anytime we have mercy, life, righteousness, and honor combined, we will have **joy**!, but that joy is rarely the product of religion. It is the product of righteousness. Through the pages of church history, those who have embraced religious rules and regulations as their security have displayed little joy. Occasionally, even singing was banned from worship sessions. Religion, with its rites, rituals, ceremonies, and sacred persons, has a way of wringing all joy from the hearts of worshippers, for joy is never the result of performance—it is always the expression of a relationship with God. The more distant that relationship is, the less joy there will be released in life. Those who seek joy as an end in itself seldom find it, but those who have learned that *"their righteousness is from Me, says the LORD,"* (Isaiah 54:17) find joy bubbling from deep within. The citizens of God's kingdom have a source of joy that the rest of the world knows nothing about, and that source is endless.

In addition to righteousness, God's kingdom is a kingdom of "peace." God's kingdom has already conquered—it is not engaged in warfare. Unfortunately, many groups of Christians do not recognize this and are continually seeking to conquer territory for God. They engage in spiritual war games and march in mock battles, but God's kingdom is amply secure. It is a peace-filled kingdom, whose king is titled *"Prince of Peace"* (Isaiah 9:6). We not only have *"peace with God"* (Romans 5:1), we have been filled with *"...peace from God the Father"*

73

(Romans 1:7), and we enjoy a relationship with *"the God of peace"* (Romans 15:33). We have been challenged to *"Let the peace of God rule in your hearts"* (Philippians 3:15), and to "Pursue righteousness, faith, love, peace with those who call on the Lord out of a pure heart" (2 Timothy 2:22).

God's kingdom is a kingdom of peace, and where peace reigns rejoicing is expressed. Peace and joy are connected for the simple reason that joy flows out of peace. Paul wrote, *"Now may the God of hope fill you with all joy and peace in believing"* (Romans 15:13), and told us that *"the fruit of the Spirit is love, joy, peace... "* (Galatians 5:22). Peace and joy go together like love and marriage.

Joy is a Phenomenon of God's Kingdom

We would be hard pressed to name one nation on the face of this earth that is filled with joy. They have their festivals and times of exuberant national expression, but true joy flowing consistently among the residents of the land is unseen. Kingdom joy is a phenomenon limited to God's kingdom. No earthly potentate has successfully duplicated this characteristic of God's kingdom.

The most obvious reason, of course, is the fact that the **force** of God's kingdom is love while the ruling force of most kingdoms is compulsion, trepidation, or injunction. God does not coerce, He comforts. He does not compel, He entices. His control is not vested in law, but in love. Like the adoring parent whose every action is rooted in love, God brings us into a joyful security by manifesting his loving nature to us in every provision, instruction, and correction.

Not only is the force of God's kingdom love, His very

government is **paternal.** The "King of kings and Lord of lords" is also called "Our Father." Repeatedly, the residents in His kingdom are called the "sons of God," or the "children of God." This kingdom is one great family. We live widely separated one from another, and our cultures and languages are different, but we are brothers and sisters in God, for we have one Father. Our commonality is not merely cultural, we have a genetic strain in the Spirit and a heritage in our life that creates a likeness to our Father and to one another. It is this family relationship that lays the foundation for such joy.

The hallmark of the Kingdom of God is **liberty.** He came *"To proclaim liberty to the captives, and the opening of the prison to those who are bound"* (Isaiah 61:2), and Jesus said, *"Therefore if the Son makes you free, you shall be free indeed"* (John 8:36). The only bonds in the kingdom of God are the bonds of love. God does not call persons unto Himself to make slaves of them. He calls slaves unto Himself to release them to complete liberty.

When former slaves receive their freedom, when condemned men are fully pardoned, and when captives are released, there is a joyful response. Look at the children of Israel dancing exuberantly on the far side of the Red Sea! Their's was the joyful song of free people. Similarly, when we realize that the power of sin has forever been broken from our lives the most natural response from within us is joy—exuberant joy!

There are those who preach a gospel of gloom and doom, but one wonders if they have ever truly entered into the Kingdom of God. There are the legalists who would extract from us every observance they think they see in the written law of God, but who want the fruit of their lives as a model for their own righteousness. Joy is a

75

strength for us, and it is a prospect, product, and a distinct phenomenon of God's kingdom. If we are in God's kingdom, can anything other than righteousness, peace, and **joy** dominate our lives?

(From *Tabernacle Tidings*)

Chain Churches

"Oh, it's beautiful in America," Hans said as he leaned back in a patio chair with a cup of coffee in his hand. Still suffering jet-lag from yesterday's flight from Holland, he hadn't slept much, but he missed nothing as his eyes swept over the backyard and enjoyed the Georgia landscape. Last evening, he had been a fountain flowing with questions as he began to savor this visit to America, but his first question this morning, as we sat beside the pool, caused me to do a double-take. "Are most of the American churches chain churches?" he asked me.

"Chain churches?" I responded.

"Yes," he answered, "like McDonalds."

Although English is but one of five language my friend speaks, he communicates well in our language, but sometimes his vocabulary is limited.

"You mean denominations, don't you?" I said.

"Yes," he said, "where they are all alike."

It has been nearly a year since that innocent remark was made, but I have never forgotten it. During the months that I have traveled since then, I am just about convinced that his word was better than mine.

Across our nation, we have chains of churches that are as alike as any of our chain stores. Their product is as interchangeable as Sears merchandise, and their spiritual food seems to have been prepared from a common recipe by cooks all trained under the same chef. Often the personnel is in the same uniform, and their communication has been memorized from the same instruction book. About the only difference that is discernible is the personality of the manager/pastor. One must read the name of the town in the church bulletin to determine where he is worshipping.

Perhaps this is not all wrong. What works well in one place is worth trying in another, and with today's rapid communication and transportation, nothing remains hidden very long. Furthermore, religion cannot live exclusively in a realm of ideas; it must have some visible status in this daily world, for the invisible Church is known through the visible Church on earth. Whether we like it or not, with our inner religious experiences come attachments to particular places, persons, times, and institutions. If these attachments are severed, the whole spiritual life may be threatened.

In working with our mobile society, all pastors have contacted families who, in moving from one location to another, seem to lose all relationship to religion because it no longer has any connection to the church where they were saved, baptized, and perhaps married. Not everyone has developed a relationship with God that is sufficiently strong to survive the loss of old ties. For them, a chain church means continuity.

Some people demand sameness in their religion. They want all the activities in the church to be called by the names they are used to, they want the same hymnal and choruses, and they even insist upon the same style organ as "in the home church." Religious experience is not an adventure for them; it is a duty, and the more it remains unchanged, the easier it is to function. For them, the strong denominational church is the answer.

But isn't there a place for difference? The strong attraction of our modern shopping centers is not merely the three or four large chain stores that form the nucleus of the mall, but the individual boutique shops, the mom-and-pop operations, and the one-of-a-kind stores. Some of these have done so well that they, too, have now become chain operations.

Every community needs a church that is different. Change is painfully slow in chain operations, both commercial and religious, but the one-of-a-kind operations can change in a moment's notice. They are able to respond to today's market rather than remain locked into yesterday's programming. This, of course, can be either a blessing or a curse depending upon the leadership and the built-in checks and balances.

The most progressive churches I have visited in the past three years do not look or act like chain operations. There is individuality, difference, freshness, and even some daring in their operation, style, and expressions. Although they seem to be aware of what others are doing, they have a vision of their own. Others may think that they are out of step, but the truth is that they are listening to a different drummer.

In examining the men and women God used throughout the Scriptures, I am convinced that God enjoys variety. Look at the tremendous contrast between meek Moses and militant Joshua, or between Peter and Paul. Even in the natural realm, nothing God created is exactly the same—from snow drops to mountains. Although there is similarity in music, each piece is distinctive. Shouldn't we allow for individuality and difference in our places, forms, and expressions of worship?

When I travel, I shun the chain restaurants. I want to experience something different—something local. As a result, I have had some very exciting gastronomical experiences, some of which were very good. The same can be said of churches I have visited.

I do not prescribe the dismantling of our chain churches. They meet a need for a large segment of our society, but I do yearn for more religious entrepreneurs who dare to be different in responding to the spiritual needs of a society that is changing faster than our religious institutions.

(From *Ministries Today*)

We Must
Maintain Balance

One of the priceless fundamentals of God's provision in His universe is balance. He ordained that light would balance darkness, water balance land, sound balance silence, and man would balance woman. Everywhere you look, God has put a balance in nature. Plants utilize the waste carbon dioxide of man and produce the oxygen so desperately needed by man. Job 37:16 asks, *"Dost thou know the balancing of the clouds, the wondrous works of him which is perfect in knowledge?"*

Whenever man has tampered with nature's balance, he has gotten himself into trouble. Australia introduced rabbits to their continent, failing to realize that there were no natural predators to keep them in balance and rabbits soon overran the country.

Balance is essential to life. "All work and no play, makes Jack a dull boy," we used to say. More eating than exercising produces an unbalanced body. All study and no social involvement produces an unbalanced person, generally unable to cope with real life.

Ecclesiastes 3:1-8 suggests that there is a time for all things and then lists them in beautiful balance: born/die; plant/reap; kill/healed; breakdown/build-up; weep/laugh; mourn/dance; cast stones/gather them; get/lose;

keep/cast away; love/hate and war/peace. One balances the other. We never live entirely in one circumstance.

Just so, balance is rudimentary and basic to our spiritual life. Job cried (31:6): *"Let me be weighed in an even balance, that God may know mine integrity."* Conduct must balance concept: John 13:17—*"If you know these things, happy are ye if you do them."* Faith must balance works: James 2:26—*"So faith without works is dead."* And law must be balanced by love: Galatians 5:14—*"For the law is fulfilled in one word even this: thou shalt love thy neighbor as thyself."*

It is dangerously simple to take one side of a truth, magnify it out of proper prospective, and develop a creed, doctrine, practice or concept based on this. Historically this has been widely practiced. The Armenians would rather fight the Calvinists than be balanced by them. The evangelical tends to scorn the liturgical as surely as the Marthas tend to berate the Marys. Yet neither is correct, because each is unbalanced.

It has been pointed out that the truth of God flows like a river, creating two banks easily identified as God's provision and man's responsibility. Through the years, men have built denominations on each bank, but the divine truth is the stream flowing between them. How sad it would be to spend our life protecting one bank or the other without ever taking a swim in the river.

A chorus that has enjoyed a surge of popularity for several years pleads:

> Cause me to come to thy river,
>   O Lord,
> Cause me to drink of thy river,
>   O Lord,

Cause me to live by thy river,
   O Lord,
Cause me to come; cause me to drink;
   cause me to live.

Obviously, none of us wants to be thought of as un-balanced. Yet, maintaining balance is a difficult chore. Do you remember walking the railroad tracks as a child? I do. At times, it required a flailing of the arms and some awkward leaning of the body to stay on that narrow rail of steel, and the game was over if we lost our balance and fell onto the road bed.

Similarly, we need consistent adjustments to maintain balance in our teaching and behavior. Sometimes we must shift our weight almost violently, but we have put our weight on God's narrow way and it is all over if we fall off. We need to keep our eyes on the pathway before us and walk carefully.

Balance is indispensable to our ability to walk, both in the natural and in the spiritual. Whether from drunkenness, drugs, dizziness or injury to the inner ear, when the sense of balance is lost, a person staggers, stumbles, circles or falls. It can be amusing or tragic depending upon our viewpoint and the outcome.

There seems to be a lot of staggering and stumbling of the body of Christ today. Something has disturbed our balance. I see people running in circles who once walked a straight line, and others are falling when there is nothing to trip over. How did we so quickly lose our sense of balance?

As children, we used to enjoy playing on the teeter-totter. We learned to balance the weight of the players by moving the lightest person farthest from the fulcrum. This enabled a very light person to balance or over-balance a much larger one. I still remember the feel of power I had if I could get farther out on the board than the other person. It was all a matter of adjusting to the balance point.

I earnestly fear that some rather lightweight truths have been moved far to the tip of the teeter-totter, thereby giving it apparent weight that it does not inherently possess. It is in control only because it has gained leverage by moving farther from the fulcrum—the Word of God.

For example, the teaching on submission seems,- in many circles, to have been shifted far out from the fulcrum. The call of First Peter 5:5—*"Ye younger submit yourselves unto the elders"* seems to have overpowered the command of James 4:7—*"Submit yourselves to God."* Wives are so pressed to *"submit yourselves to your own husbands"*(Ephesians 5:22) that we ignore: *"We ought to obey God rather than man"* (Acts 5:29).

It seems that in order to control the teeter-totter, some have shifted their emphasis out to the extreme end; all the while they are gently pushing the opposite view closer and closer to the fulcrum. What then appears to be balanced is actually badly out of balance in relationship to the fulcrum. While it is a valid Scriptural teaching that we: *"Obey them that have the rule over you and submit yourselves"* (Hebrews 13:17), it is going far beyond the truth to say we should obey them blindly in matters contrary to the Word, good sense and decent morality.

Yet, such imbalance is being taught by some. They say we are not responsible for either the validity of the command or the results, that our only responsibility is obedience. One such person jeopardized my life with this teaching. He had been sent to pick me up at a major city airport after an unforeseen snow storm had made it impossible for me to fly into his town. The man's elder had instructed this disciple to bring me, no matter how bad the road conditions became. I insisted that a phone call be placed to him describing how treacherous the roads were, but the response was simply to come on and he would accept full responsibility for the consequences. The disciple was again instructed to drive me through if it took all night, for I was the first speaker of the conference.

After we had spent two or more hours going less than ten miles, I insisted upon one more phone call. The disciple was very reluctant to do so, arguing that if he obeyed his headship, God would see them through. Although the disciple agreed that it was dangerous and foolish, he had his orders and intended to follow them.

I still insisted on one more call, so he pulled into a motel to make the call. While he phoned, I registered my wife and myself into a room, took a shower and went to bed. By the time the driver found me to tell me his orders were still to "press on," I was comfortably drifting off to sleep.

The disciple who obediently went on, spent the night gaining less than twenty miles. The next morning the storm was over, the road had been plowed open and we drove safely and comfortably on; arriving within two hours of the disciple who had obediently gone on.

While I believe in submission and headship, I don't enjoy having a man sit comfortably in front of the fireplace in his home playing God with my life. He may have been willing to accept responsibility, but I was the one they would have buried.

Some wives are being taught such extreme submission to the will of their husband, that if the husband requires the wife to prostitute herself, she has no right to question him. They are told that he will be responsible before God. DON'T YOU BELIEVE IT! No matter what the husband may tell her, she has to give account of her actions before almighty God (Romans 14:12—*"So then every one of us shall give account of himself to God"*). Simply pleading: "My husband ordered me to do it" will no more excuse her than Adam's plea, "the woman you gave me, she gave me...".

Some elders are exercising control over the lives of submitted "disciples" as to totally control their expenditure of personal finances, what kind of car they can drive, who they can date or marry, what churches are to be visited, etc. Haven't we learned, by now, the difference between submitting in love one to another and controlling one another? Jesus forbids His disciples from exercising lordship over one another: Matthew 20:25-26—*"Jesus said, ye know that the princes of the Gentiles exercise dominion over them, and they that are great exercise authority upon them. But it shall not be so among you:* but whosoever will be great among you, let him be your minister."

What shall we do? Knock submission off the balance board? No! Let's put it back in an honest relationship to the fulcrum—the Bible. Ephesians 5:21 says: *"Submitting yourselves one to another IN THE FEAR OF GOD."* Here is the scriptural balance. We are to humble ourselves one to the other while being balanced with our reverential fear and respect for God and His will as revealed by the Spirit and the Word. We do not simply submit to God THROUGH His man, as some have taught, but submit to God AND His man, in that order.

I find no difficulty in submitting to a man who is properly submitted to God, for I am first of all submitting to the same Lord and find we are working under the same orders.

Young's Concordance defines the Greek word *Hupotasso,* from which we get the word "submit" in the

New Testament, (with the exception of Hebrews 13:17), to mean: "to set in array under." When I am in a church, I am happy to set the ministry "in array under" the local pastor. I will observe his "no no's" and follow his lead. When I am in a conference, I take my headship from the conference directors. I do not desire to violate local headship. But my submission ministerially does not give them "lordship" over me. There is but one Lord and we are under His orders first and finally.

Imbalance seems to be intrinsic to our fallen state. The pendulum swings from one extreme to another. Yet Solomon tells us: *"A false balance is an abomination to the Lord"* (Proverbs 11:1). We must maintain the integrity of the individual believer as a balanced teaching on "submissions," "discipleship," "covering," and "divine order." Remember that *"The head of every man is Christ"* (I Corinthians 12:3), and we are all *"a royal priesthood"* (I Peter 2:9); being made *"kings and priests unto God"* (Revelation 1:6). As such, we have unlimited and open access to the Father. While the Lord has given us godly elders to hear the voice of God WITH us, they are not given to hear the voice of God FOR us. The undershepherds are not expected to replace our sensitivity to God, His voice and His leadings, but to be checks and balances in our walk with God. They are assistive— supplemental, but not substitutive. Any who would seek to be a substitute to God will be confronted with the jealousy of God.

I, too, want to see an end to lawlessness, rebellion, undisciplined behavior and kingdom building. But let's not create one evil to deal with another. Anarchy has been a consistent enemy of and in the church through the ages. Let's not strengthen it to overthrow a vocal minority who have appeared to prefer to go their own way.

87

Let's resist becoming extreme, unbalanced, in any teaching or practice. Let's again put our feet on God's narrow rail, balance our weight, and carefully *"walk in the Spirit, and ye shall not fulfill the lusts of the flesh"* (Galatians 5:16).

(From *Praise Digest*)

The Believer
in Worship
The Feast of Passover

Ask any ten Christians about the origins of the feast of Passover, and it is likely that nine of them will refer to the incident in Egypt when God passed over the homes upon which the blood had been applied. However, it is probably more accurate to say that this incident marks the point at which the feast took on a commemorative aspect as well as a cutting of covenant with God. There are scholars who are convinced that the feast of Passover had its beginnings with Adam's family in their observance of God's command to offer the firstborn of the animals unto God as a sacrifice. Abel brought the firstlings of his flock as an offering to God, while Cain brought only the fruit of the ground. That the firstborn belong to Jehovah is a primitive ordinance, and this custom can explain the remarkable choice of the plague smiting the firstborn of Egypt.

When we remember that Moses' request of Pharaoh was to allow the children of Israel to go into the wilderness to offer a sacrifice unto the Lord, taking along their cattle and sheep, we can easily assume that the Israelites were eager to give the firstborn back to Jehovah, for their slavery had prohibited such sacrifices in Egypt. Pharaoh's consistent refusal to allow this sacrifice provoked Jehovah to take the firstborn of the Egyptian households as a substitute. Since it was commonly thought of primitive peoples that the firstfruits of life in any sphere belonged to God or the gods, Jehovah's taking the firstborn was viewed as evidence that the gods of Egypt could not protect the Egyptians' oldest sons. This contributed to the people's willingness to give propitiatory offerings of gold, silver, and jewelry to the Hebrews while actually hastening them out of the land of Egypt.

In the Passover, we probably have one of Israel's oldest feasts. At least it is the only one represented in the Old Testament as established before the Exodus. This feast was so well known to the Hebrews that Moses did not have to give many explanations about it when he implemented it before the Exodus. What he apparently did was to adapt a recognized feast to commemorate a divine deliverance. This adaptation was so thorough that the memorial aspect of this feast overshadows the covenantal aspect of it in most of our minds. It is another example of God taking what was well known and using it to teach what was, at that time, totally unknown. In remembering this feast, we might increase our appreciation of it by viewing its prophetic, practical, preservative, panegyric, personal, and perpetual aspects, for the feast of Passover encompasses all of these.

Passover is Prophetic

Since Pharaoh would not allow the Hebrews to offer the firstborn of their flocks to Jehovah as a covenantal sacrifice, God declared that He would take the firstborn of the land as a substitute. Nonetheless, the Hebrews lived

90

in the land with the Egyptians, and their firstborn were as much in jeopardy as those of the Egyptians. Unless some provision of exemption was made, all firstborn males would die on the night of God's visitation, but because God's judgment was lovingly tempered with mercy, a way of escape was provided for the "whosoever." This exemption gave the permanent name of "Passover" to the existing feast connected with the offering of the firstborn unto the Lord.

Moses taught the Hebrews of God's instructions to declare the current month as the first month of the year, and in anticipation of what was to come, they were to take, on the tenth day of the month, lambs according to their families. If the family was too small to dispose of a lamb, two or more households could unite for this festive celebration. Either a lamb or a kid could be taken, but it had to be a perfect animal—one year old. This separated animal was to be kept until the fourteenth day of the month, and then the head of each household was to slay his lamb at the evening hour. After catching the blood of the sacrifice in a basin, he was instructed to take hyssop, a very common plant in Egypt, and stain the lintel and doorpost of the house in which the feast was to be held, which, if the basin was placed in the doorstop, would form a bloody cross on the doorway. This became the outward sign that separated the faithful from the fearful—that signified to the destroying angel that this household was to be exempted from the decreed judgment of death.

Inside this sanctuary, the sacrificed lamb or kid was to be eaten with unleavened cakes and bitter herbs. It was to be roasted intact with head, legs, and innards, and everything was to be eaten in haste; the participants were fully clothed and packed for the exodus. Anything uneaten was to be burned before daylight.

91

The Hebrew word that we translate as "passover" is *pesah* which comes from the root *pasah*, meaning "to pass" or "spring over" or "to spare." Some have suggested that when God went through the land destroying the firstborn, He passed over (skipped over) the houses that were marked with the blood of the covenant. Other Bible scholars point out that God would have commissioned an angel to this slaying, and that God Himself passed over these consecrated dwellings in the sense of making a tent of His presence over those houses. No plague can overcome the one who abides in the secret place of God's presence. The covenant of blood secured a covering of God's presence; God passed over His people as a mother hen gathers her chicks under her wings in the time of danger.

In saying that the Passover was prophetic, we are merely declaring that before it came to pass, God declared that it would happen, and He described ways and means of securing safety in the hour of judgment. It was one of those prophetic exhortations and provisions that had such an immediate fulfillment as to inspire faith both in God's Word and in His leadership. Just as Jesus told His disciples, "I tell you these things before they come to pass that when they come to pass you may believe," so God delights in forewarning His people so that they may be forearmed against the day of calamity. But for us Christians, there is also a far more reaching prophetic implication than these Hebrews could have envisioned. It speaks plainly to us of Christ becoming our paschal lamb, Whose blood applied to our lives and homes has secured the same safety in the hour of judgment as these Hebrews enjoyed. *"When I see the blood I will pass over you..."* (Exodus 12:13) is as real in the twentieth century as it was in the days of Moses.

92

Passover is Practical

God knows better than we do that involvement is a necessary expression of faith. Rather than have the Hebrews sitting around fearfully waiting for the destruction that had been prophesied, God gave them something constructive to do while they waited. They had a lamb to slay, blood to sprinkle, a feast to prepare, a journey to pack for, and a meal to be eaten in an attitude of haste. Everyone was a participant in these activities, and it kept the family united and active as a unit. The household was not totally dependent upon the father's faith, for their participation required personal faith from each member.

Furthermore, the activity God chose afforded strength for the journey that was before them, for they were about to escape God's judgment, and they were escaping over 400 years of slavery. They were headed for an entirely different form of life, and the initial step from being Egypt's slaves to God's freedmen was going to be exhaustive. This hot meal served the immediate purpose of providing strength for their pending journey. Is anyone more practical than our God?

A third practical function of this passover celebration was that it gave occasion for rejoicing among the Hebrews while there was extreme anguish in the Egyptian households. The mourning of the Egyptians could hardly be heard in Goshen for the singing and rejoicing of the Hebrews when the blood caused God to pass over them. Their jubilation began the very hour that judgment fell on their enemies.

Joy and rejoicing have always been God's antidote to fear and anxiety. We are challenged to feast and rejoice in spite of the condition of the world, for we are here on a very temporary basis. The day of our deliverance will soon come, too!

93

Passover is Preservative

God commanded that Passover be a perpetual feast. This exploit of God's deliverance of the Hebrews from judgment, bondage, and Egypt was a one-time act of God that was to be told to their children and their children's children. To help perpetuate the memory of this deliverance, God made Passover a commemorative feast for all generations and connected it with the week-long feast of unleavened bread. Although the slaying of the lamb was no longer to be done at home, it was still to be performed by the head of the household at the Temple, and all the rest of the activities remained family-oriented. It was to be a time of retelling the story of God's passing over the households marked with blood, of the angel of judgment passing over these houses over which God had made a tent of His presence, and of the Israelites passing over the Red Sea.

Furthermore, it was a constant reminder of a covenant that had been made with God. By a covenant of blood, they had reaffirmed God's ownership of all the firstborn, both human and animal. This first Passover had returned the Hebrews to a covenantal relationship with God that had been affirmed to Abraham. In their annual observances of this feast, there was both a reminder and a renewal of this covenant. Just as a wedding ring reminds a couple of covenants made years ago, so this feast reminded Israel of a covenant relationship they had entered into with their God. God was *their God*, and they were His people.

Because memory is so fickle, God often set festival memorials and sacraments as reminders of past victories He has given to His people. Israel did not walk in perpetual victory, and neither do we. While we do move from faith to faith, there is often a fight between these levels of faith. In the midst of the conflict, we need to be reminded of God's past interventions on our behalf, for past victories produce present faith. *"Hitherto hath the Lord helped us..."* (I Samuel 7:12) is as faith-inspiring today as it was when Samuel declared this. While we should never look back to the pit from which we were delivered with any desire to return, we do well to regularly look back at the great deliverance God wrought on our behalf. We cannot live in memories of the past, but we should not try to live without memorials to past victories. The Passover, and the subsequent Lord's Supper, are faith-producing memorials every believer needs. *"Forget not all His benefits...",* the psalmist declared (Psalm 103:2).

Passover is Panegyric

This seldom-used word simply means "a formal public eulogy" (*Funk and Wagnalls*) or a "festival assembly" (*Webster*). Although the feast of Passover remained a family activity—prepared and eaten in individual households—it was governed by divine regulations and entered into on the same day, and the sacrifices were made in large gatherings at the Tabernacle and later, in the Temple. Once this nighttime feast was consumed, the feast broadened into a full week of celebration that took on a very festive air. After leaven was searched out, the emphasis was upon feasting, not fasting, and song and dance were the order of the day. They were commemorating a victory, and they did it joyfully and jubilantly. In eulogizing God's great Passover, the Hebrews struck the vibrant chord of joy with a festive atmosphere and pleasant memories.

Sometimes I wonder if our celebration of the Eucharist hasn't become too solemn and formal. We seem to commemorate the agony and shame of the cross even

95

more than we do its victory. Do we celebrate the pain or the purpose of the cross? Are we merely commemorating the death of the Son of God, or are we celebrating the vicariousness of His blood applied to our lives which has given us eternal victory over death? Passover was a feast—a panegyric celebration. Victory was memorialized in annual celebration. Isn't it still beneficial to simply celebrate God?

Rejoicing, not remorse, was the order of the day, and it is still the correct way to commemorate God's victories in our lives. God has turned our mourning into dancing, our sorrow into joy, and our fear into faith; He has given us a gift of joy, a fruit of the Spirit which is joy, and has made us participants in His kingdom, which Paul describes as *"joy in the Holy Ghost"* (Romans 14:17). The worship of the Old Testament was joyful; surely the worship of New Testament saints should not be less exuberant and fun-filled!

Passover is Personal

Of the seven feasts of Jehovah, none was more personal than the feast of Passover. It was the only feast in which the head of the household was commissioned to slay the sacrifice. All other sacrifices were slain, prepared, and offered by the priesthood. Furthermore, this was the only feast that was celebrated in the homes by family units. Since the feast was as much covenantal as it was commemorative, God ordained that its observance be limited to the family unit, for God always sealed His covenants with families and then let the families make up the nation. Perhaps in America's church orientation, we have side-stepped the family unit, but God views His Church much as He viewed His nation of Israel—a gathering of families into a collective body. There must remain some celebration of God that is family-oriented and home-oriented. Traditionally, the celebration of the Lord's Supper has become a collective ordinance for the entire congregation to participate in together, but in the beginning it was a memorial kept by the family unit. Unfortunately for our generation, we have not replaced this family feast with another form of commemoration of God's great deliverance from sin. Even the family altar seems to have passed away.

Salvation is a very personal act; it is a one-on-one involvement with a person and his God. It was the father of the household who applied the blood in Egypt, and it is still an act of an individual to apply the saving grace of our Lord Jesus Christ. Since the act of salvation was such a personal work, should not the celebration of that act also become a very personal response? Perhaps the local congregation can be viewed as a family unit, but the celebration should have a personal involvement that goes beyond the corporate function. It was for *me* He died, so I should be the one to celebrate this deliverance.

Another peculiarity of the feast of Passover that makes it a very personal feast is that it was a nighttime feast—the only nighttime feast Jehovah provided. It was celebrated at night since that was the time when God's judgment was poured out upon the firstborn of the land. Emotionally, that was a night of darkness, dread, fear, and anxiety, and life still has many dark night seasons in it—times when we sit fitfully wishing for the day. Anxiety is usually connected with the unknown, and we live facing great unknowns. In the daylight these factors seem quite harmless, but in our night seasons—those times when we are less aware of the presence of God—the unknown quotients can haunt us like the proverbial ghost in the cemetery.

97

How did God handle their night season? He gave them a victory celebration to be observed in the darkness of night. God has not promised us perpetual daylight, but He has provided songs in the night. Families can draw close together in seasons of darkness, and God has even provided a feast for the nighttime hours. Unquestionably, we sense loneliness more in the nighttime hours than during the activities of the day, so God provided at least one great feast to be celebrated by families who are experiencing the loneliness of death, separation, tragedy, or simple insecurity. The feast is a reminder that we are not in the night hours alone—the Lamb of God is there at the feast with us. We need not fear what the darkness can bring to our families, for God has made a protective tent of His presence over us—He has promised to "passover" us. We celebrate this in faith and great joy even in the hours of darkness.

Passover is Perpetual

Since the real purpose of Passover was to glorify the God of Israel and to attest God's gracious act of leading His people from bondage to freedom, it is to be expected that it would become a perpetual celebration, for each succeeding generation needs to be reminded of the grace of God that was demonstrated to their forefathers. With some modifications, this feast is still celebrated by Jews throughout the world. The slaying of the lamb and the sprinkling of blood on the doorway have been discontinued, but the rest of the feast remains very much the same today. It is historic, covenantal, and commemorative of the greatness of God on behalf of His chosen people.

Nonetheless, the Jews are not the only people to perpetuate the memory of Passover. Zondervan's *Pictorial*

Encyclopedia observes that "the Passover is equally important to the synoptic gospels; so much so that it is possible to view the gospel of Mark as a Christian Passover."

When Jesus used the paschal meal for the occasion of the Last Supper, He reinterpreted the Passover in terms of the Messianic event, and the Messiah took the role of the paschal lamb. In this sense, at least, the Last Supper provides Passover with a new content. To the church at Corinth, Paul wrote: *"For even Christ our passover is sacrificed for us: therefore let us keep the feast..."* (I Corinthians 5:7-8). When we substitute the Lord's Supper for the Passover, we need to remember that Passover was a memorial meal that brought them into a fresh covenant with Jehovah. Both Luke and Paul speak of the memorial aspect of the Eucharist in reminding us of the words of Jesus: *"This cup is the new testament in my blood"* (Luke 22:20).

We Christians need to be aware of the difference between the sin offering, which was totally burned and never eaten, and the paschal lamb, which was eaten entirely. The Passover was not directly concerned with sin; it was concerned with covenant. For the Hebrew, eating the paschal lamb never meant eating his God; he was simply cutting covenant with his God through the sacrificial route. Such eating of the sacrifice was a joyous occasion and gave cohesion to the community life. As Zondervan's *Pictorial Encyclopedia* observes:

> For this reason, the emphasis in the Last Supper must be placed as much upon the Covenant as upon the sin offering, if not more so. The blood that sealed the Covenant is not the blood poured upon the

altar, but the blood sprinkled upon the people. The Covenant is at the core of the Passover account. On the eve of the Exodus, God revealed Himself as the God of the Fathers who remembered His Covenant (Exodus 2:24; 3:15). On the eve of the Crucifixion, this covenant was reaffirmed by the Messiah's willingness to shed His blood. The paschal lamb is therefore not sufficient to explain the full meaning of the Last Supper; the Covenant intrudes as the over-arching theme.

The Last Supper actually continues the Passover theme in the fresh context of the work of Christ in that it is a memorial feast of the Person and the work of Christ, it is a pledge of loyalty between Christ and His disciples, and it reaffirms the covenants of God and seals them in the blood of Christ Jesus. Furthermore, it expresses the joy of salvation and the awareness of Christ's triumph.

In bringing Passover from the Old into the New Covenant, we go beyond moving from political to spiritual, for the Passover is the beginning of a journey that Christ completes by reaching the goal. Jesus completes what Moses began, but could never accomplish in the ultimate sense, for true freedom is freedom from sin. No one is truly free who is a slave to sin. Only the one whom the Son makes free is free indeed (see John 8:34). The Exodus had a limited goal, which was not reached until a new generation grew up. It is but a parable of man's journey into the Promised Land. But the New Covenant in the blood of Christ brings us beyond the parable to practical participation in freedom in Christ. We have passed from death into life, from sin unto salvation, and we are now living as God's freedmen in His earthly kingdom.

Passover commemorates the historic Exodus, which was limited to the experience of one generation of a single race of people. The Christian Exodus, under Christ, is open to the nations of the whole world throughout the entire span of time. "Whosoever will" is the call of the Christian Exodus. That which began in Egypt will continue into eternity without the limitations, frailties, and failures connected with the first Exodus. Having moved from shadow to substance, we are assured of complete victory all the way into heaven. We will "passover" to the other side.

(From *Times of Refreshing*)

Rewards of Remembrance

Scientists tell us that every impression made upon the human brain is there for that person's lifetime, but the ability to recall this information is extremely limited—in fact, most of us use no more than ten percent of our brain's capacity. Our ability to function in life is very dependent upon our recall faculties, and thus loss of memory means the loss of ability to function in or relate to that area of life. Unfortunately, our propensity to forget greatly exceeds our ability to remember.

David wrote, *"Bless the Lord, O my soul, and forget not all His benefits"* (Psalm 103:2). David directed his intellect and emotions [soul] to recall, review, and recite God's past blessings so that he would *"forget not all His benefits."* Long before pedagogy [teaching] became a science, David established that review is the first law of learning, but while we know this to be true in secular learning, we often fail to apply it to spiritual truth. In our quest for the new, we often fail to review the old and thus lose from our recall faculties the foundational truths that we learned through God's dealings many years ago. Of God, David said, *"I remember you on my bed, I meditate on you in the night watches"* (Psalm 63:6). David knew that to review is to renew.

103

Remembrance Blesses the Lord

But rehearsing to imprint truth in the conscious mind wasn't David's exclusive reason for remembering the goodness of God. He felt that such remembrances actually bless the Lord, for that is the theme of Psalm 103. It begins and ends with "Bless the Lord, O my soul!" The Lord is blessed when we joyously talk of the past goodness of God.

Many modern Christians major so much in the present as to feel guilty when looking at the past, but everything is an eternal "now" in God's sight; it is we who divide life into past, present, and future. Praising God for what He has done blesses Him as much as praising Him for what He is presently doing. Again and again, the prophets called for Israel and Judah to remember God's past benefits to them and to respond to God accordingly. The Spirit still challenges us to bless God by remembering what He has done for us in past days. Actually, it is only the redeemed who want or dare to look back at their past!

Remembrance Removes Regret

Solomon ended the book of Ecclesiastes with the admonition, *"Remember now your Creator in the days of your youth"*(Ecclesiastes 12:1), and then he proceeded to graphically describe old age clear to the point of burial. Perhaps he wanted to emphasize the shortness of life and urge the youths to enjoy God to the fullest while they still had the chance. But he might also have been implying that the older we get, the less we want to remember "the former days," for all of us have failures, sins, disappointments, sorrows, and "skeletons in the closet" upon which we choose never to reflect.

David seemed to be aware of this, for immediately after

commanding his soul to *"forget not all His benefits,"* he reminded himself that the Lord *"...forgives all your iniquities...heals all your diseases...[and] redeems your life from destruction"* (Psalm 103:3-4). David dared to look backward, for all of his confessed sins had been forgiven, canceled, and blotted out.

For the converted, remembrance removes regret. Our memory circuits maintain a consciousness of the act, but the grace of God has removed the sting of guilt and the stain of the sin. When memory rehearses our failures, we rejoice in God's forgiveness and the knowledge that He crowns us *"with lovingkindness and tender mercies"* (Psalm 103.4). Remembrance need not return guilt; it restores confidence in God's cleansing. We do not remember with remorse; we remember with rejoicing.

Remembrance Reinforces Faith

Remembrance actually reinforces faith by strengthening truth. Peter did not seem to consider his books to be revelation so much as reminders, for he wrote, *"...in both of which I stir up our pure minds by way of reminder"* (2 Peter 3:1). Saints don't necessarily need new truth; they merely need to have the truth renewed, and memory is an amazing tool for reliving past experiences and rekindling present faith.

When God had Israel in the wilderness, He told them, *"If you should say in your heart, 'These nations are greater than I; how can I dispossess them?'—you shall not be afraid of them, but you shall remember well what the Lord your God did to Pharaoh and to all Egypt"* (Deuteronomy 7:17-18). God's challenge was for them to use their memories to inspire courage and confidence for the future, very much as Samuel set up a memorial stone after his first victory over the Philistines and called it

105

"Ebenezer", meaning: "Thus far the Lord has helped us." This memory aid inspired faith when the enemy attacked in the years that followed. Every Christian needs a few "Ebenezer stones" in his memory circuits as positive reminders of God's past intervention of grace on his behalf, for confidence is built upon experience.

Remembrance Reinstalls Caution

Confidence isn't the only thing that memory can build, for an active remembrance reinstalls caution. Remembering the pain of a burn keeps our hand off a stove. This is why Jesus told the Pharisees, *"Remember Lot's wife"* (Luke 17:32). We will not live long enough to learn everything through personal experience. Happy is the person who can learn through observation, for remembering the result of the action of another can prevent a similar personal sorrow.

Although in some Christian circles there is great emphasis upon the healing of the memories, there is much in our memories that God wants to leave untouched, for these memories of hurt, sorrow, pain, and separation are consistent deterrents to repeat performances. God told Israel, *"You shall remember that the Lord your God led you all the way these forty years in the wilderness, to humble you and test you, to know what was in your heart, whether you would keep His commandments or not"* (Deuteronomy 8:2). Remember the tests, and you may not have to repeat them!

Remembrance is Reciprocal

Remembering all God's benefits becomes a reciprocal action, for as we remember God, He remembers us! The prophet wrote, *"Then those who feared the Lord spoke to one another, and the Lord listened and heard them; so a book of remembrance was written before Him for those who fear the Lord and who meditate on His name"* (Malachi 3:16). God gave us the book we call the Bible, but He has two personal books in heaven. One is called *"the Book of Life"* (Revelation 3:5); the other is this "Book of Remembrance," which contains the names and conversations of those saints who use their memories to talk to one another about the Lord. *" 'They shall be Mine,' says the Lord of hosts, 'on the day that I make them My jewels' "* (Malachi 3:17).

Rememberers are not only remembered; they become rejoicers, for having spoken of God's greatness to Him in the past, David cried, *"Sing praise to the Lord, you saints of His, and give thanks at the remembrance of His holy name"* (Psalm 30:4). Remember, rejoice, and give thanks!

(From *Harvest Time*)

107

Christian Meditation

When David wrote, *"Give ear to my words, O LORD, consider my meditation"* (Psalm 5:1), he obviously coupled prayer and meditation, but in the succeeding generations, the two seem to have been divorced. It has been many years since I have heard a sermon on meditation, and it is a rare Bible dictionary or encyclopedia that even lists the word any more. Meditation has been replaced with activation. Modern religion is far more concerned with doing than with thinking. Nevertheless, there can be no such thing as neutral thinking.

In Romans 8, Paul established that the mind-set of an individual controls his life.

"For those who live according to the flesh set their minds on the things of the flesh, but those who live according to the Spirit, the things of the Spirit" (Romans 8:5). Paul made it abundantly clear that the way one thinks is intimately related to the way one lives, and he declared that the set of the mind determines life or death and warfare or peace with God (see verses 6-9). Little wonder, then, that we are commanded to *"set your mind on things above, not on things on the earth"* (Colossians 3:2).

Meditation Duplicated
One of Satan's favorite tools is error by excess. He long

ago learned that the Church almost instinctively reacts to overemphasis with de-emphasis, so he has frequently caused Christians to abandon vital truth and practice by introducing an excessive counterfeit that distorts the plain and pollutes the pure. He has never been more successful at this than in making the very word "meditation" distasteful. To most Christians, the word brings up images of practitioners of yoga sitting cross-legged in a self-induced trance, or of persons mindlessly chanting their secret mantra in the practice of transcendental meditation. The more this counterfeit has been commended in our universities, the more meditation has been censured in the Church, but a counterfeit only reaffirms the value of the real; it should not become a replacement for the true.

Meditation Defined

Withdrawal from life in monasticism is not the scriptural concept of meditation; savoring of life through meditation better fits the Bible view. As the Lord said to Joshua, *"This Book of the Law shall not depart from your mouth, but you shall meditate in it day and night, that you may observe to do according to all that is written in it. For then you will make your way prosperous, and then you will have good success"* (Joshua 1:8).

Two separate Hebrew words are translated "meditate" in our English Bibles. *Hagah* literally means "to ponder or imagine." It is the word used in the beginning of the Psalter: *"But his delight is in the law of the LORD, and in His law he meditates day and night"* (Psalm 1:2). The other word is *siyach*, which means "to converse with oneself aloud, to commune, or to muse." It is used repeatedly in Psalm 119—*"I will meditate on Your precepts, and contemplate Your ways."*

In the New Testament, Luke and Paul used the Greek word *metetao* (which means "to resolve in the mind or to imagine") when they spoke of meditating. Paul told Timothy to *"meditate (metetao) on these things; give yourself entirely to them, that your progress may be evident to all"* (1 Timothy 4:15).

Meditation is Desirable

It is self-evident that the scriptural concept of meditation is not mindless muttering of memorized mantras, but it is reflecting, pondering, contemplating, imagining, and even conversing on a selected subject. It is not mental relaxation; it is mental activity.

This could be one of the reasons for the decline of meditation in our society, for we are not a thinking generation. We give ourselves to amusement rather than to meditation. "Muse" means "to think," and "a" is a Latin prefix that means "not"—so amusement is "not thinking," and how we Americans surround ourselves with amusements. If that isn't sufficient to keep us from thinking, we turn to alcohol or drugs to alter the action of our minds. One wonders if life has become so miserable that people do not want to think about it. Perhaps our generation has everything with which to live, but nothing *for* which to live.

This is not true of praying Christians. We not only have a hope of a bright future life, but we have been made partakers of Christ's life in the nasty here-and-now. We live in sweet communion with Jesus Christ, and He stimulates our minds with His love and provisions. David declared, *"When I remember You on my bed, I meditate on You in the night watches" (Psalm 63:6), and "I remember the days of old; I meditate on all Your works"* (Psalm 143:5).

111

The Discipline of Meditation

Meditation is a very rewarding prelude to both prayer and worship, for it brings spiritual renewal and mental refreshing, and it opens the door to Divine communion. He who prays without first meditating usually prays by rote or unto himself. Communication with God must begin first in our thought patterns, for it is imperative that our minds be running before we put our mouths in gear if we plan to have any forward progress.

Prayer is a response to God in His Word, in His saints, and in His heaven, but that response cannot be higher than our concepts of God; therefore, any enlargement in our prayer lives demands an enlargement of our views of God. Concepts do not come out of casual observations. They require concentration, thought, and meditation. This is not an instant process; it requires time. It has been said that new ideas or truths must be reconsidered daily for at least twelve days in order to be indelibly retained in the mind. Truth is lost unless it is mentally reviewed, renewed, and responded to. This is where meditation best serves the believer.

Meditation is not mindless seeking or self-awareness, nor is it aimless reaching into the spirit world. It is conscious, concentrated thinking on a chosen subject. When that choice is God's Word, works, wonders, and world, it enlarges our concepts of God, encourages our faith in God, and enhances our responses to God. Meditation becomes a private devotional act that is deliberate and continuous. Whenever the conscious mind is not occupied with the duties of the day, our thoughts can be turned to meditating on the things of God, and this often becomes a silent prayer of our spirit.

A sweet prayer, and so spiritual that it is used almost as commonly in Christian worship as is the apostolic benediction, comes from the meditation of David. He wrote, *"Let the words of my mouth and the meditation of my heart be acceptable in Your sight, O LORD, my strength and my redeemer"* (Psalm 19:14). The separation has lasted long enough. It is time that prayer and meditation get married again!

(From *Charisma*)

Practicing the Psalms

Psalm 5

"Whatsoever he saith unto you, do it" (John 2:5).

Is it possible to have come through the soul searching of the Watergate revelations with the subsequent investigations of the FBI, the CIA and other governmental agencies without asking yourself, "How can I prevent similar wickedness in my own behavior?" Jeremiah quoted God as saying: *"The heart is deceitful above all things, and desperately wicked: who can know it?"* (17:9). None of us really knows what is in our heart until pressure, tension or opportunity causes it to reveal itself.

In the fifth Psalm, David suggests three actions that will prevent wickedness, in its varied forms, from lodging in the heart. Three things that will purify our motivations so we need not fear life's manifestations. In verse 2, he says: *"I will pray"*—in verse 7, he declares, *"I will worship"* and in verse 11, he pledges, *"I will rejoice."* After each promise, he gives his reasons, always prefacing them with the word "for." Look at them.

First, he says, *"I will pray"* (vss. 2-3) and then in verses 4-6, he lists seven things God detests, starting the list with the preposition "for," inferring that by praying he would prevent any of these things from taking root in his life.

Only the upward look of prayer and the communion with God it affords can ever prevent these actions, so very common in life, from controlling us.

The list is formidable: (1) Wickedness (Heb. "moral wrong"), (2) Evil (Heb. "to break to pieces; destroy"), (3) Foolish (Heb. "boasters"), (4) Iniquity (Heb. "nothingness, specifically an idol"), (5) Leasing (Heb. "lying"), (6) The Bloody Man (Heb. "lover of violence"), (7) Deceit.

In a permissive society such as ours, only prayer will prevent the decay of our morals, deliver us from self-destruction, temper our boasting, preserve us from idolatry, seal our lips with truth, keep our hearts from violence (even the vicarious violence of TV) and cause us to walk honestly. No wonder David declared: "I will pray."

But as valuable as prayer is, it is not the total answer. In verse 7, David pledges, *"I will worship"* followed by a list, in verses 9 and 10, of five things worship will prevent. It is possible to pray from a distance, but worship demands an entrance into God's presence, so David says, *"I will come into thy house...and I will worship."*

Worship brings us into a much closer relationship with God than prayer alone does and allows God a more intimate relationship with us. It is during times of worship that deep inner cleansings and changes occur. Isaiah (ch. 6) was cleansed when in the presence of God and we can be also.

David suggests that worship will prevent: (1) Faithlessness (v.9), (2) Inward wickedness (immoral desires), and (3) Inner filth ("open sepulchre"). The Living Bible translates it: *"Their suggestions are full of the stench of sin and death,"* (4) Flattery, and (5) Rebellion against God (v.10).

Whereas prayer dealt with actions, worship deals with attitudes. Prayer changes manifestation, but worship commutes motivations. As I pray, I am able to conform to the will of God, but as I worship, I am transformed into the image of God. Paul declares this in 2 Cor. 3:18, *"But we all, with open face beholding as in a glass the glory of the Lord, are changed into the same image from glory to glory, even as by the Spirit of the Lord."* Beholding His image, we are changed into that image. No wonder Jesus said that the Father was seeking worshippers (John 4:23).

David's third positive action was to rejoice (v.11). The Amplified Bible translates this action very positively: *"Let's all...rejoice; let them ever sing and shout for joy...let those also who love your name be joyful in You and be in high spirits."* In the last two verses of this psalm, David suggests that rejoicing in the Lord will provide at least three positive actions on God's part. First, *"Thou defendest them"* (v. 11). The Amplified Bible says, *"You make a covering over them and defend them."* Hallelujah! God makes a tent of His presence over the rejoicing saint as secure as was His covering over the Hebrews on the night of the slaying of the first-born sons. My rejoicing invites His covering, and His covering inspires my rejoicing.

Secondly, David assures us that shouting for joy causes God to bless the righteous (v.12). All of our pleading for God to bless us, bless the food, bless the offering, bless our ministries go unheeded. If we want God to bless us, we need only to start rejoicing in Him, shouting His praises, singing unto Him. He responds to rejoicing by letting His blessings flow.

Finally, David assures us that when we rejoice in the Lord, He will "Compass" (Heb. "Crown") us with favor and surround us as a shield. Divine protection from head to foot and from front to back is offered to the rejoicing, praising, shouting, joyful saint. How natural, then, that Paul so repeatedly challenged the Christians to *"Rejoice*

117

in the Lord; and again I say, Rejoice." (Phil. 4:4). "I will pray—I will worship—I will rejoice."

(From *Praise Digest*)

Magnify the Lord

"Let all those that seek Thee rejoice and be glad in Thee: let such as love thy salvation say continually, The Lord be magnified" (Psalm 40:16).

This beautiful and inspired utterance from David's heart has been set to music and is now sung by worshipers throughout this land. The unusual wedding of words and music produces an emotional response in me every time I sing it. And yet, in the midst of this beauty and excitement, it is possible to miss the real teaching of this verse. It is a summary exposition on *praise*. It is concerned with the Alliance of Praise and the Ardor, Antiphony and Ascent that praise should produce within us.

The Alliance of Praise
"Let all those that seek thee..."

Webster defines *alliance* as being "a connection between families or individuals or union by relationship in qualities." Although praise is often a private response, in the Scriptures, it is far more often a public act of worship. The work of Christ at Calvary has produced divine qualities in the lives of believers that has blended them into a homogeneous unit variously referred to as "a family, a bride, a body, a church, or a royal priesthood." Whatever collective noun is used, it is always God's

119

possession. It is "the family of God, the bride of Christ, the Church of God," etc. We are not an organization united by common goals, but an organism actuated by a common life. The psalmist is not so much speaking of a group of petitioners united to curry favor from an omnipotent king as he is alluding to a segmented whole reaching toward God as its only hope of unity, much as a magnet can unite metal filings.

Praise, then, is first a recognition of an alliance between an individual and his God. God is the head, he is the body. God is the source of life, he but the expression of that life. As the person sees the tremendous availability of God to his life, praise rises in his bosom as naturally as the morning rising of the sun. When, however, he sees beyond the availability of God, to the reality of God, praise explodes within him as the only meaningful response to the presence of a living God.

Soon, however, the praiser finds that he is not alone. There are countless thousands of "seekers after God" who also emote their feeling into praise at the conscious awareness of His divine Presence. Their common nature, common need and similar experiences form a strong alliance between them that gently brings them out of "singular praise" into "united praise." Their common bond becomes a basis for a common song. The Bible is filled with the musical praises of united congregations of people. If we are *seekers* together, we will be *finders* together and cannot help but be *responders* together. Our alliance with Christ has formed an alliance with brethren that has become a glorious alliance of praise!

The Ardor of Praise
"...rejoice and be glad in Thee."
Too many people seem to think of praise as merely an

120

attitude. They are more given to pondering than to praising. They are more "thinkful" than thankful. But as surely as thanksgiving demands an action (the actual giving of thanks), so praise demands an expression of inner attitudes.

Here the psalmist calls for two actions. First, *rejoice.* Secondly, *be glad.* The Hebrew word for "rejoice" is *soos,* which literally means "to be bright, cheerful or to make joyful mirth." The Hebrew word for "be glad" is *samayach,* which means "to be gleeful, joyful, or making merry." To the merely religious person this is near sacrilege. They equate sobriety and silence with worship. Not so the Scriptures. The Old Testament times of worship were fun-filled festivals. There was the solemn ritual and ceremony of the sacrifice, but once they were assured of God's acceptance of the required gift, they took the remainder of the offering for a picnic or party. It was a time of merrymaking, mirth, singing, dancing, laughter and fellowship. That was God's way. What a pity we have so changed it in our generation.

Some time back, while ministering in Australia, I picked up a foreign edition of the *Reader's Digest.* In it was a short item telling of a man commissioned to take a traffic survey at a busy intersection of one of our major cities. He observed that on Sundays, people walking to the downtown church were thoroughly enjoying themselves and one another until they approached the front of the church, at which time they became rigid, formal, sober and quiet. At the conclusion of the service, they came out of the church very pious and formal and remained this way until they had crossed the street, at which time they seemed to relax and begin to fellowship with one another normally. He asked the question, "What goes on in the American church that so deprives

121

people of all joy and normal responses to life?" It's a noteworthy question.

Here the psalmist suggests that the united seekers after God should brighten up, be cheerful, be glad, even mirthful. We are not headed for a funeral, but a resurrection. We are not walking into darkness, but into *"marvelous light."* We are not coming before our judge with hearts full of guilt, but before our Father with hearts full of love. We are not even coming to petition, but to praise Him for His marvelous works, ways and personage. This is festive day, not a day of fasting. We have come to celebrate Divine victory, freedom, promise and community. We have reason to be bright and cheerful —*"Let us Rejoice and Be Glad in Thee."* Those who know not God may weep, mourn, be pious and quiet, but those who have come to know their God personally will brighten up, be cheerful, gleeful, joyful and make mirth in a merry way. This is the expression of Praise's Ardor within us.

The Antiphony of Praise

"....let such as love Thy salvation say continually..."

Antiphony is simply a responsive alternation between two groups, especially singers. The angels in Isaiah's vision, chapter 6, seemed to be calling antiphonally one to another. As we come into the presence of God through worship, He speaks to us. It may be through His Word, through prophecy, by the inner voice of the Spirit, or through preaching, but we become aware of God's speaking. Our proper response, our antiphonal response, is praise. How the Psalms are filled with such responses! Repeatedly, following a recounting of something God said to David, David cries, "Therefore will I praise Him." Little wonder, then, that he repeatedly writes, *"O, that men would praise the Lord."* It is the verse the master songwriter wrote and set to music. It is what the choir director is trying to get from us. God does His part very well. The next step is ours. It is a response of praise. Sing it, shout it, say it, show it, dance it, clap it, and whisper it, but express it somehow. We are to say **continually...**"

The Ascent of Praise

"....the Lord be magnified."

The Hebrew word for "magnified" is *gadal*, which literally means to enlarge by twisting (as in making of a rope), but in normal usage means to be made large or cause to be made large.

In Psalm 34:3, David cried out, *"O magnify the Lord with me."* But how can we magnify or enlarge God? Obviously we cannot. He already fills the whole universe. But we can magnify our concepts of God. We can increase our perspective of Him.

When viewing scenery, it is not too uncommon to put a pair of binoculars to our eyes to "magnify" some specific item. What we do, actually, is block out the foreground, eliminate the background and optically bring the object closer to our vision. It enables us to see in detail as though we had moved much closer. It this not what this verse is requesting? "Point your binoculars on God." Block out the foreground and eliminate the background that so often distract our attention from God. "Zero in" on God. Bring Him into focus once more. Get you eyes off the *gifts* and the *ministries* and fix them on the *giver* and the *man Christ Jesus.*

Praise is the finest set of binoculars God has given us. When we are praising in depth, we are like the three disciples on the Mount of Transfiguration after the voice of the Father had spoken. We *"see no man save Jesus*

123

only." Praise causes us to get so caught up with the person of God that we aren't unduly distracted with the program of God. Praise magnifies God to our vision, making Him nearer and dearer to our lives.

On the wings of praise, I can ascend into the presence of God, for it is His required means of entrance. With the vision of praise, I can see into the nature of God far more clearly. With the vocalizing of praise, I can release my deepest feelings of love and adoration unto my gracious Lord and Savior. Therefore, *"Let such as love Thy salvation say continually, The Lord be magnified."*

(From *World MAP Digest*)

124

The Highway of Holiness

When Paul made his defense before King Agrippa, he declared that the work of Christ and the spread of the gospel *"was not done in a corner"* (Acts 26:26). The work of God is not done behind closed doors, for God's goal is to reveal Himself to this world, not to conceal Himself from it.

Furthermore, God loves to state His purposes in advance of His performances. It is His joy to alert His Church on earth to the plans being laid in heaven. He spoke through Isaiah, encouraging us to expect some revelation of coming events rather than to live entirely in the past: *"Behold, I will do a new thing, now it shall spring forth; shall you not know it? I will even make a road in the wilderness and rivers in the desert... to give drink to My people, My chosen. This people I have formed for Myself; they shall declare My praise"* (Isaiah 43:19-21).

Occasionally when God does a "new thing," it appears as dramatically as the opening of the Red Sea, but most of the time God prefers to work progressively, as in the production of a rose. Step by step and process by process, God brings forth His predetermined purposes in the lives of persons and in His corporate Church on earth. Sometimes the individual steps are so supernatural when compared to our time/space experience that we mistake the process for the product. Too often, it is our hindsight that enables us to see that God was at work in a continuing pattern.

One wonders if this might be the present attitude of the Church as she views the Charismatic renewal which God poured out on His people. It is common, now, to speak of that visitation of God in the past tense, and many writers are asking what tangible and permanent results are to be found. Wouldn't it be easier to find answers to such questions if we viewed the Charismatic renewal as part of a process rather than as the end result of a process?

God's Kingdom is Now

One of the emphases in the Charismatic renewal was a rediscovery of God's kingdom here on earth. We heard much about recapturing the arts and sciences for Christ. We were taught at length about our authorities here in this life and our proper relationships one to another in the light of Christ's earthly kingdom.

Isaiah also got a glimpse of God's kingdom on the earth, and in Chapter 35 of his book, he described some of the glory that would be manifested when that kingdom was in authority. Isaiah viewed it as future, and more and more Christians are becoming aware that the beginning of that fulfillment is upon us. The best is yet to come, but the beginning has already arrived. Christ's pattern of prayer is being fulfilled: *"Your kingdom come. Your will be done on earth as it is in heaven"* (Matthew 6:10).

The Dead Church Revived

The prophet saw the necessary progression in bringing the kingdom of Christ into operation here on this earth, and he listed at least seven steps in its fulfillment. His **first** assertion was that a dead Church would be revived, for he proclaimed that *"the desert shall rejoice and* *blossom as the rose; it shall blossom abundantly"* (Isaiah 35:1-2). This blossoming is connected with great rejoicing in verse two.

This is something we have already witnessed in the Charismatic renewal. Churches that were virtually lifeless began to flower with praise, rejoicing, and singing. Praise characterized this renewal even more than the operation of the gifts of the Spirit. It was a singing renewal, and the exuberance of the renewed Christians manifested itself in a great variety of ways, but all of them were joyful. This explosion of rejoicing brought the beauty of flowering roses to congregations that had been dependent upon mental pictures of past seasons of blessing. We no longer need to talk about "the good old days," for the best days of our lives were being lived enthusiastically. God was present, and His people were praising Him. Deserts became rose gardens.

The Ignored Christ Seen

The **second** step Isaiah spoke of shows that an ignored Christ was finally seen in His Church, for he wrote, *"They shall see the glory of the Lord, the excellency of our God"* (Isaiah 35:2). Most congregations had seen programs, personalities, and problems for so long that they had forgotten what the glory of the Lord was like. During the renewal, our attention was focused on Christ in all of His beauty, and *"we beheld His glory, the glory as of the only begotten of the Father, full of grace and truth"* (John 1:14).

There is a magnificence in the glory of the Lord that cannot be compared to anything else in life. God's glory not only came to His people; it was placed in His people, and its transforming power caused the inner glory of God to radiate in the outer manifestations of lives. Even the world had a chance to see the glory of God in the lives of believers.

Weak Saints Strengthened

Some of the results of seeing this glory were described by Isaiah as a strengthening of the weak hands and a firming of the feeble knees (see Isaiah 35:3). The **third** step God used was to strengthen His weak saints. Those unable to serve because of weakness in their hands were strengthened to give both to God and to others, and the Christians whose knees could not bear them in their daily walk were given renewed ability to *"walk in the Spirit"* (Galatians 5:16). The Charismatic renewal released many thousands of Christians into Christian service beyond anything they had ever experienced, and it picked up the feeble saints and strengthened them to walk in the Lord as maturing adults.

The Fearful Made Fearless

Coupled with this **(fourth step)** was the command to *"say to those who are fearful-hearted, 'Be strong, do not fear!' "* (Isaiah 35:4), and the reason given for fearlessness was the promise that *"your God will come with vengeance . . . and save you"* (verse 4). Oh, what boldness accompanies every move of the Holy Spirit, and what boldness we saw in the Charismatic renewal. The cowardly became courageous; the fearful seemed to be fearless. The presence of the Lord in His glory always removes fear and restores confidence. God's faith in Himself and His Word is infectious to those who get close to Him.

Deformed Saints Healed

The **fifth** action of God that Isaiah saw in preparing God's people to enter into the kingdom of God here on earth was a marvelous wave of healing that would restore the deformed to wholeness. Isaiah said, *"Then the eyes of the blind shall be opened, and the ears of the deaf shall be unstopped. Then the lame shall leap like a deer, and the tongue of the dumb sing"* (Isaiah 35:5-6). This speaks of complete restoration of the capacity to see, to hear, to walk, and to speak. What a glorious fulfillment of this that we experienced in the Charismatic renewal, both spiritually and literally. The presence of God among His people gives us a spiritual vision that enables us to see into realms to which we have been consistently blind. It opens our ears to hear spiritual things to which we were formerly deaf, and it enables us to walk in paths that were too difficult for us in our lame condition. Furthermore, God unloosens our tongues to declare what we have seen, heard, and walked in.

In the days of Jesus, He walked among the lame, the deaf, and the blind at the pool of Bethesda, but healed only the lame man among them; but in the days of the renewing of the Church, Christ Jesus is opening the eyes, ears, and mouths as well as healing the lame. God is restoring our full spiritual faculties in the moments before we come into a complete revelation of His kingdom on earth.

Productivity That Perpetuates

The **sixth** step in God's process is a restoring of the land to fertility. Isaiah said, *"There shall be grass with reeds and rushes"* (verse 7). God first restored beauty in causing the desert to blossom with roses, but here He restores utility in giving the grain and grass needed for the continued sustaining of life.

The prior work of God was to bring His people out of the despicable condition into which religion, without

129

relationship to God, had plunged us, but here God purposes that the maturity we have entered can continue to bring forth life-giving and strength-producing grass to perpetuate what He has done. We always appreciate God's rescuing acts, but often we expect Him to repeat that action to sustain what He has saved. His consistent program, however, is to mature His people so they may sustain the work that He has begun.

Following the dramatic rescue and subsequent rejoicing of His Church, God led His people into a time of intense teaching and training to induce growth unto maturity. Some rejected it while contending for a continuation of God's first visitation; completely ignoring the fact that what is brought to birth must also be brought to maturity so that it can, in turn, bring to birth in its own right. Some groups have embraced this action of God beautifully, while others have rejected it ultimately.

The Final Move

It is the **seventh** step in this process of God that seems to be the current urging of the Holy Spirit. Isaiah defined it as *"a highway...and a road, and it shall be called the Highway of Holiness"* (Isaiah 35:8). The land is fertile, the flowers are fragrant, and the people are formidable, so God purposes to build a roadway through it into His presence—a roadway He chooses to call "the Highway of Holiness."

The construction of roadways is always costly and difficult. There will always be citizens who object to the route that is chosen, while others declare flatly that the road will destroy the natural beauty of the land. This is never more true than when applied to the spiritual world. When God renews His people and their land, most Christians are comfortable with the results and are

130

content to live in this splendor without change "until Jesus comes," but God's goal is to bring heaven's authority back to the earth to make the heavenly and the earthly kingdoms function as one. This requires quick and direct access between God and His people, and Isaiah likened this access to a highway. God wants to be able to get to us quickly and have us get to Him easily. A highway is the answer.

A Highway of Holiness

If God were asking for the construction of a freeway of service, sacrifice, or silver, the Church would gladly build it for Him, but God is asking for a Highway of Holiness, and in general the Church is afraid of holiness. Our fear is based on a faulty definition of holiness, but holiness is not the way we live; it is the life we live.

God alone is holy. God is ultimately holy. God is intrinsically holy. All of our attempts to emulate this are doomed to failure from the very beginning. Nothing we can do can transform us from our basic unholiness into God's pure holiness. Generations of persons have made themselves miserable trying to achieve this holiness through their self-denial and self-righteousness, but it only produced spiritual pride.

Holiness is God in Us

Becoming holy is not a self-help project; it is a Divine work requiring a Divine enabling and human coopera- tion. If holiness is the essential nature of God—and the angels proclaim that it is—then living in holiness is living in the nature of God, having holiness is having the nature of God, and becoming holy is becoming like God.

When Peter quoted from the Old Testament: *"Be holy, for I am holy"* (1 Peter 1:16), he was offering us a

131

commitment from God, not merely a commandment from God. How merciless it would be for God to command us to be what we cannot inherently become. God declares that He is willing to make His holy nature available to us through the Holy Spirit. Holiness is positive, not negative; it is progressive, not instantaneous, and its source is Divine, not human. Holiness is a power rather than a persuasion; an enablement rather than an emptying. Holiness is not an abandoning of self so much as it is a receiving of Christ's life into ourselves.

The holy person will be clean, moral, upright, and honest in his behavior, but these traits are mere evidences of his holiness, not the producers of it, for there are clean, moral, upright honest persons who are not holy people at all. Living at the zenith of earth's standards cannot produce the indwelling, divine life of Christ, but God's indwelling, holiness will lift us to the zenith of God's standards for behavior. Holiness changes our inner desires, which in turn control our outer deeds, for all the actions of the holy person reflect changed attitudes rather than controlled behavior.

A Limited-Access Road

This route into the presence of God that the Holy Spirit is now building in Christ's Church on earth is not intersected by multitudinous crossroads, nor is it interspersed with traffic signals. It is a freeway—the King's highway—that can be entered only at Divinely placed cloverleafs. Isaiah declared that *"the unclean shall not pass over it...no lion shall be there, nor any ravenous beast go up on it"* (Isaiah 35:8-9). Nothing that threatens the security of the believer is granted access to this highway of holiness. Instead, *"Whoever walks the road, although a fool, shall not go astray"* (verse 8). This route into the divine

132

Presence is a protected, exalted, and patrolled road that is reserved for the exclusive use of the redeemed, as Isaiah foresaw: *"... the redeemed shall walk there"* (verse 9).

It has been puzzling to many pastors to see many who were renewed of the Holy Spirit turn aside when God began to build this highway of holiness. Perhaps they failed to recognize the difference between the outpoured rain of the Spirit upon the dry land and the indwelling reign of God in His people. First God revives, and then He regulates. He begins by inspiring happiness, and then He implants holiness. He calls to Himself before He seeks to control us.

Holiness is not the joy of birth; it is the fruit of maturity. The spiritual baby who is still wearing diapers and eating Pablum is not expected to be holy, but the maturing adult who is walking with God is brought from the nursery to the highway, and a higher form of life in God is entered into.

Historically, Christians do not want to grow up. We love the attention that babies and children get, and we become so dependent upon others doing for us that we refuse to take our rightful place in Christian society as producers and doers unto others. We prefer the playground to the highway of holiness, but God's kingdom cannot be run from the park; it requires involvement with the world around us in commerce, education, politics, the arts and sciences, marriage, and so on. When God begins to move His Church into the "real" world, many of its members retreat to the sandbox, where they can play spiritual games until supper time; but God is building a highway of holiness that will quickly transport His people from His presence to the four corners of the world as representatives of God and His heavenly kingdom.

133

Conclusion

Isaiah concluded his progressive vision of God involving His people in the affairs of the world by saying, *"And the ransomed of the Lord shall return, and come to Zion with singing, with everlasting joy on their heads. They shall obtain joy and gladness, and sorrow and sighing shall flee away"* (Isaiah 35:10). There is no hint that the highway is restrictive; instead, it seems to release God's people to rejoicing. The way of holiness is a shortcut into God's presence—why wouldn't we rejoice!? This highway of holiness is a place of absolute protection, and that alone should inspire song. The road of righteousness is a route to productivity, for holiness produces results in this life on earth as well as in eternity.

Roads are not built merely for motion; they are built to speed transportation from point A to point B. God is building a highway of holiness in His Church on earth to move us rapidly from where we are to where He is. Therefore, holiness is never punitive; it is productive, and the greater the level of holiness, the greater the level of productivity in the things that affect God's kingdom here on earth. Those who resist the present work of the Holy Spirit to induce holiness in their lives will again find themselves mired in the marshlands of religion; those who submit to the gentle workings of the Spirit inducing God's holy nature into them will soon be moving on God's highway of holiness that spans the distance between the kingdom on earth and God's kingdom in heaven.

(From *Life in Christ*)

Silence or Shouting?

In the outpouring of the Spirit at the beginning of this century, there was a great division among the recently Spirit-filled believers over the way to express worship. Some thought that enthusiastic, demonstrative praise was God's highest order for their lives, while others insisted that quietness was more consistent with the nature of God. Out of this conflict, the hymn "Blessed Quietness" was born and, so I am told, became the dividing line in the revival that God was sharing with His Church on earth. How sad that it had to become an "either/or" instead of a "both/and" situation, for worship is the joyful response of a believer to his God, and each of us is highly complex with varying moods. We have seasons when we are very outgoing and gregarious, and we also have times when we are personal and quiet. Worship that is real, in contrast to ritual worship, will, of necessity, be expressed in a way consistent with the mood of our inner nature at that given time.

Quietness in Our Private Lives

As meaningful as talking is, as communication and as the basis for interaction with other people, there comes a time when a person needs and desires to be alone with himself. God told Israel, *"In quietness and confidence shall be your strength"* (Isaiah 30:15). Inner strength

135

demands some quality quiet time. All of us need time for reflection on the many inputs the world has made to our lives in any one day, for we have been stimulated mentally, visually, aurally, and through our other senses, but we often have not taken the time at the moment of stimulation to fully savor and learn from these inputs. A quiet time at the end of the day enables us to contemplate the situations we have encountered in the preceding hours and to discern those things that need to go into our memory circuits.

Quietness in our private lives enables us to get further input into our minds through reading, radio, and television. It is a time when we are not having to communicate back; we're merely receiving input and deciding what to do with it. Quiet times also afford seasons of amusement. "Muse" means "to think," while the prefix "a" means "without"; hence, amuse literally means "without thinking," and all of us need times when our minds do not have to think. Sessions of "not thinking" often release communication from our subconscious minds which gives us input that has been gathered more from what was sensed than from what was said. All too frequently this gentle input is crowded out by an overactive mind.

Depending upon the nature of our life's work, quietness may occupy a greater or a lesser portion of our time. The teacher will spend most of the day talking, while the accountant will be thinking. However, it is possible for that talking teacher to experience quietness, while the accountant may be fighting a storm within himself, for quietness is more than the absence of speech; it is the absence of inner tension. Paul exhorted Timothy: "...*that supplications, prayers, intercessions, and giving of thanks be made for all men, for kings and all who are in authority, that we may lead a quiet and peaceable life in*

136

all godliness and reverence" (1 Timothy 2:1-2), and Peter spoke of *"the incorruptible ornament of a gentle and quiet spirit, which is very precious in the sight of God"* (1 Peter 3:4).

Quietness in our public lives often comes as the result of discipline. It is not always opportune to release our true feelings, and our ideas or suggestions may be unacceptable in many situations. Our relationship with our fellow employees may tend to be disturbing, but we learn to maintain our "cool" in spite of their prodding. Paul, in talking about brotherly love, wrote, *"We urge you, brethren,... that you also aspire to lead a quiet life, to mind your own business, and to work with your own hands, as we commanded you"* (1 Thessalonians 4:10-11). This may not be innate, but it is achievable; we can learn to be at peace inwardly even in the midst of a storm.

Quietness in Our Worship Experience

Response to God in a worship experience calls for reflection on the goodness, the nature, the character, and the promises of God. Meditation is a necessary prelude to worship, and it is frequently done in the inner quietness of a person's spirit. When an awareness of God has been quickened and we respond in worship, we often come to the highest level of worship, which is adoration, and this may be a very quiet, contemplative, loving expression. True worship will have its times of quietness.

Man Shouting from the Housetops

This expression comes from the Phillips' translation of the words of Jesus: *"Whatever you whisper within four walls will be shouted from the house-tops"* (Luke 12:3, The New Testament in Modern English). Christ's basic message is that nothing can be kept secret for very long.

137

This is fundamentally true of all of us. What works inwardly in our quiet times, comes outward in our more gregarious moments. Inner questions often builds tension that can best be released by outward proclamation, for Jesus Himself declared, *"Out of the abundance of the heart the mouth speaks"* (Matthew 12:34).

Shouting in Our Private Lives

Shouting in our private lives is often necessary as an expression of jubilation. Some levels of joy just cannot be expressed with a whisper or a quiet word, as is evidenced at any ball game when the hometown team scores. Life needs its shouts to maintain emotional equilibrium. The Psalms abound with exhortations to *"let them shout for joy and be glad"* (Psalm 35:27). Joy is such an important part of our nature that God gives it to us as a gift, includes it as a fruit of the Spirit, and promises to increase it to us (see Isaiah 9:3, for instance). Joy needs to be expressed to be fully savored.

Shouting in Our Public Lives

Joy and joyful experiences are not entirely private. Our interaction with others is often the source of our highest joys. Sharing life with others is often the source of our highest joys. Sharing life with others amplifies our feeling of elation. A sunset viewed alone isn't nearly so impressive as when its beauty can be shared with another, and the release of excitement by the solitary person watching a football game on television isn't even close to being as demonstrative as that expressed by the fans in the stadium. The very sharing of life will induce seasons of jubilant shouting.

There are other times when we must shout merely to be heard. With so many voices in life, quite frequently only the loudest ones can be heard. We raise our voices in frustration, anger, and excitement because we want to be heard rather than ignored. Life the brokers on the floor of the stock exchange, we will do whatever is necessary to be heard.

Shouting in Our Worship Experience

Most people are more familiar with quietness in worship than with shouting as part of worship, but over sixty-five times, the Bible speaks of shouting as an acceptable part of our worship response. In Psalm 47, the psalmist talked about God ruling the nations as *"the King of all on earth"* (verse 6). He began the Psalm with *"O, clap your hands, all you peoples! Shout to God with the voice of triumph!"* (Psalm 47:1). Just as surely as there are experiences in our natural lives that cannot honestly be responded to with anything less than a shout, so there are spiritual experiences that demand the emotional release of the shout. The prophet exhorted, *"Cry out and shout, O inhabitant of Zion, for great is the Holy One of Israel in your midst"* (Isaiah 12:6). He understood the need for releasing joyful emotions unto God in an enthusiastic manner.

Both Quietness and Shouting Are Natural and Necessary

While it is obvious that some people seem to have quieter natures than others, it is both natural and necessary for the quiet person to have times of shouting and for the shouting person to know times of quietness. God does not prefer silence above shouting, or vice versa, nor does He reject either one, for He is not deaf, nor is He nervous. The choice of expression is less what pleases God and far more what is honest to our inner feelings. God desires to be worshipped *"... in truth"* (see John 4:23-24).

139

This means more than mere correct words—it calls for correct emotion in expressing those words.

"Blessed quietness?" Yes, *and* blessed noise. Meditation and contemplation are part of the real "us," but so are singing, shouting, dancing, and praising. All that God really wants from us is that we "be real" in expressing ourselves before Him.

(From *Harvest Time*)

The Believer
in Ministry

Grumbling, Gathering,
and Grinding

I have repeatedly declared that most of the problems we have encountered in the Church and in every move of God could have been averted if we had been faithful students of history. The human heart is the same everywhere, and Satan has no new tactics available to him. When writing to the church at Corinth, Paul commented concerning the Israelites, *"All of these things happened to them as examples—as object lessons to us—to warn us against doing the same things; they were written down so that we could read about them and learn from them in these last days as the world nears its end"* (1 Corinthians 10:11, *The Living Bible*). The man who insists upon learning everything by personal experience will either not survive long or will never progress very far, for he insists on starting over rather than beginning where another has left off.

Right now in the body of Christ there is a tremendous emphasis upon "faith," but most of the emphasis seems to

be "faith for things" rather than "faith in God." We are being taught formulas that are supposed to coerce God into giving us exactly what we want, when we want it, and in the quantity we want. The will of God does not seem to be a contributing factor; it is the will of the individual that is supreme. Assuming the formulas to be workable, are they also practical? Is it good for us to get our own way simply because we demand it? Is it true that we know what is best for our lives, or could the old-fashioned concept that God knows what is best for our lives be safest?

The Old Testament has abundant answers to this. One of them is found in Chapter 11 of the book of Numbers. The chapter begins, *"When the people complained, it displeased the Lord: and the Lord heard it; and his anger was kindled."* That anger was manifested in a destroying fire that probably would have annihilated all of them had not Moses interceded before the Lord on behalf of the people. One might expect that such instant and pestilential judgment would end complaining about the ways of the Lord, but by verse four of the same chapter we read, *"And the mixed multitude that was among them fell a lusting: and the children of Israel also wept again, and said, Who shall give us flesh to eat? We remember the fish, which we did eat in Egypt freely; the cucumbers, and the melons, and the leeks, and the onions, and the garlick: But now our soul is dried away: there is nothing at all, beside this manna, before our eyes"* (Numbers 11:4-6). In spite of God's discipline they were still self-centered and inherently selfish.

The Grumbling About the Manna

Whenever there is a mixture, you can expect trouble. This mixed group likely consisted of Egyptians and many other races who had migrated into Egypt during the

142

famine, about the same time that the Hebrews had arrived. They had become convinced of the reality of God during the plagues upon Egypt, and subsequent to the slaying of all the firstborn in Egypt, they chose to "tag along" with the Hebrews as they followed God into the wilderness. Although they were not covenant people, God mercifully made provision for them for the full forty years of their wandering. Even so, we have no record of any of them entering into Canaan! It seems that their conviction of God's power never became a conversion to being God's people!

What sorrow we could save ourselves if we could learn from this that there is no room in the program of the Church for the unregenerate church members. They may well be convinced of God's power, but unless they are soundly converted by that power, they will be a dangerous mixture for the true Church. They may desire Christian fellowship, but they will constantly campaign for the best of Egypt *plus* the best of Canaan. They will not embrace the teaching of Jesus that it is an "either/or," not a "both/and" teaching since He taught: *"Ye cannot serve God and mammon"* (Matthew 6:24). Much church strife is directly traceable to the active participation of untransformed people, both men and women, who are convinced, but not converted! The New Testament teaches that we are either children of God who are committed to walk in His pathway, or we are children of the devil, following his will. For both to try to walk together is an improbability, and that for a very short duration of time. The ways of the flesh will not long submit to the ways of the Spirit of God, for they are in constant warfare one against the other (see Galatians 5:17).

The problem in this mixed multitude in Moses' day was

143

their differing appetites. Appetite is largely determined by family background; the Egyptian yearned for leeks and garlic, while the Israelite accepted the Divine manna. It's like a group of American tourists who make a beeline for a hamburger stand upon arrival home from travels abroad; they have been well fed, but the appetite for hamburgers and french fries has become nearly insatiable.

In the life of a believer, lust for old pleasures is a temptation of Satan. In the wilderness, the manna was available in the cool of the morning, but back in Egypt the melons and cucumbers were eaten in the heat of the day for their cooling effect. Now as the desert heat burned mercilessly upon these nomads, they remembered the temporary, but blessed relief of Egypt's cooling watermelons. The memory was natural; Satan merely amplified it into temptation which, when yielded to, became the sin of lusting. They lusted for some of the good things of the old life to the point of forgetting the slavery and terrorism that went along with it. And so do we!

Although we have been taken from the world, it is to be expected that occasionally we will have a pleasant memory of some of the activities. Merely entering the sanctuary does not cause us to forget all of the old days as if they had possessed no pleasure whatsoever. Old tastes will revive. Sometimes the mere sight of an old companion may drive one to wish for just one more day in the house of bondage. The odor of a drink or a cigarette may quicken a long-suppressed appetite, and a particular face in the crowd may awaken within one those influences which had been supposed dead. Flashing lights, the tune of a dance band, a sensuous picture, or time spent with an old photo album may quicken a desire for a short return to days in Egypt, but these memories of mind are normal, not sinful. It is human nature to remember the good and forget the bad of the past. It is likely that at one time or another, all of us have had strong yearnings to turn back the calendar of time. The danger is that Satan is quick to use these latent memories as temptation to sin, and he uses them to create dissatisfaction with our present circumstances. He wants to convince us to return to Egypt's brick kilns, and to that end, he will fill our minds with these memories, knowing full well that *"as he thinketh in his heart so is he"* (Proverbs 23:7).

This sort of thinking eventually leads to grumbling, for a strong desire for things of the past is automatic evidence of dissatisfaction with the present. When the multitude lusted for the food of Egypt, they were judged for discontent with God's manna, since discontentment with the provision and promises of God is the blighted fruit of a doubting soul. We, as they were, are the objects of God's love; God has accepted the responsibility of providing for our needs, but when we reject God's provision in preference to what has been provided in times past, we seriously endanger our relationship with Him.

This has been flagrantly evident in the past few years as God has poured out His Spirit upon all flesh. It seems that the Spirit hardly establishes residence in the lives of many before they begin lusting after a new thing. They run after any new prophet who comes on the scene, and insistently trade the written Word of God for the philosophy of man because it seems to be more palatable. They yearn after that which appeals to the carnal rather than that which appeals to the spiritual. They seldom pray, but they will tour the nation in search of a man with the gifts of the Spirit. They want the melons and cucumbers, but they disdain the solid food. In choosing what they lust after, they have rejected what God has provided, but if they are

145

going to successfully cross the desert, they had better learn to eat the food of the desert—manna—for leeks, onions, and garlic will not get them through.

The Gathering of the Manna

When it first appeared, God's food supply was an amazing miracle to the more than four million people out in the wilderness. So inconceivable was this provision that they called it "manna," which merely means "What is it?" They never did successfully define this food, nor could they store it for future consumption. Every day they had to exercise faith that God had once again met their needs. Inasmuch as they had to gather it before the sun waxed hot in the morning, and since it always came down outside the camp itself, many in the inner perimeters of the camp probably began their trek to the "manna field" in the early dawn, and they could not tell until they arrived outside the camp if the manna had fallen during the night. This called for an exercise of faith in God's provision.

It also called for an acceptance of God's provision, for while the mixed multitude stood around grumbling and lusting for the food of Egypt, God's chosen people simply accepted His provision of food and daily gathered it. How many today sit around waiting for a better pastor, a new evangelist, or a mighty moving of God while others simply go to the Word regularly and take what they need for that day. God's ministers are not the divine source of daily manna; God's Spirit and His Word are. Those unwilling to feed at God's table will have to go hungry, no matter how ominous their lust for a different fare may become. If we will not feed in God's pasture, we must either get out of it or starve, for no change in doctrine will force God to give us something beyond His present provision. Happy is the Christian who has learned to accept what God has provided.

But acceptance, as a mental acquiescence, is not sufficient, for there is need for active cooperation. Just as Israel could not produce manna, God could not gather it! The manna was not placed in their larders; it rested upon the dew outside of the camp. Ungathered, it melted in the heat of the sun. Similarly, we cannot ignore Bible reading and prayer and expect to have spiritual nourishment, for God will not do for us what He has commanded us to do. It is not without significance that Paul wrote to Timothy urging him to *"study to shew thyself approved unto God..."* (2 Timothy 3:15), for there is ample spiritual food available to us every day, but we must gather it before it will do us any good. *"The soul of the sluggard desireth, and hath nothing: but the soul of the diligent shall be made fat,"* Solomon wrote (Proverbs 13:4).

If God's manna isn't worth the effort of gathering, we'll simply have to go hungry while dreaming and longing for melons and cucumbers, but we should remember that while six Egyptian foods were listed in their lusting, God had promised them that seven foods were awaiting them in Canaan (see Deuteronomy 8:8). Since six is the number of man, while seven is the number of perfection, it becomes obvious that it is better to gather manna today while awaiting Canaan's perfect provision tomorrow than to reject today's manna while longing for the imperfect supply offered yesterday by man in Egypt.

Some of the saints who have overcome a lusting for what God has provided still live short, unsatisfied lives simply because they are unwilling to gather what is available. They do not search the Scriptures or apply faith to the Scriptures that they do search. None of us lives up to the full potential that is available to us in God's Word.

147

Perhaps we expect the food to be delivered to us by ravens, as it was to Elijah, or we may think that our cruse of oil will never fail, as in the days of Elisha, but God's provision for our spiritual nourishment is on a day-to-day basis. He grants it; we must gather it.

Furthermore, gathering manna required an embracing of God's mercy and faithfulness, for although they grumbled and lusted for some other provision, God did not measure His faithfulness to them by their faithfulness to Him, and "God changeth not." We should never fail to gather manna today just because we rejected it yesterday; God has provided manna for us today in spite of our attitudes and actions of yesterday. God's infinite wisdom knows what man needs even when man doesn't know his own need.

Not unlike the patient parent who insists on a balanced meal for his child whose only desire is for sweets, God has provided a continual supply of needed manna, for He knows that our greatest need is Jesus even while we are lusting for programs, pageants, and contests! God's supply is based neither on our worthiness nor on our wantonness; it is based both on God's faithfulness to give and our willingness to gather. If we will go to the field when the dew is upon the grass, we will find manna waiting to be gathered, for God's Spirit *(dew)* is the Divine agent for making the written Word become a life-giving word to our inner man.

The Grinding of the Manna

The grumbling mixed multitude had come to despise the manna, complaining about its sameness, but God had provided that this heavenly food on which angels feed could be ground, beaten, baked, made into cakes, or seethed (see Numbers 11:8; Exodus 16:23). Just because

148

there was but one food provided did not mean that it always had to look, feel, and taste the same, for this manna was adaptable to the satisfaction of all appetites. Its preparation was limited only by the skill and experience of the cook. Both my wife and I were raised on potatoes, and they have formed a basic staple in our home. In her kitchen, my wife has a cookbook entitled *101 Ways to Cook Potatoes*, and I would suppose that during our forty-seven years of marriage, she has served potatoes most of those ways.

Since Jesus declared, *"I am the living bread which came down from heaven"* (John 6:51), it is obvious that the manna was a clear type of Jesus Himself! Christ Jesus came to meet every need in the life of the believer. He is the perfect food, and as both the living and the written Word of God, He is available daily to satisfy every desire, fulfill every appetite, and meet every need of the redeemed. Christ is adaptable to every human need, for whether "ground, beaten, baked in pans, seethed, or made into cakes" Jesus is "all that I need." Paul declared this to the church at Corinth when he wrote, *"But of him are ye in Christ Jesus, who of God is made unto us wisdom, and righteousness, and sanctification, and redemption..."* (1 Corinthians 1:30). When correctly appropriated, Christ will be strength in the midst of weakness, health in the time of sickness, the way of escape in the moment of temptation, joy in the hour of sorrow, peace in the day of tempest, salvation in the time of judgment, wisdom in the moment of ignorance, guidance in the season of perplexity, and wealth in the period of poverty.

Since it was Christ Himself who made the great variety in our appetite structure, surely He has provided in Himself a way to satisfy each of them, for there are seven

149

distinct moods of the Spirit, which surely are enough to completely fulfill every mood of man. When we attempt to stereotype Christ and our responses to Him, we greatly limit the infinite variety that is available to us in His nature and His person. One day Christ may seem like an Elder Brother; the next day He may be viewed as the infinite God. Today He's the Saviour; tomorrow, the Judge. Now He is the Comforter; later He is the Confidant. Monday, He is the Source of our joy; Tuesday, He is our Strength amidst grief. One moment, He is our bleeding Redeemer, and the next moment, He is our guiding Light. Whatever our need, whatever our desire, whatever our hunger, whatever our appetite, "Jesus Christ is made to me all I need, all I need," a hymnist wrote long ago.

These are changing times, but God has offered us an unchanging Christ as the daily manna supply for our sustenance. If we will gather and grind that manna, we will *"be strong in the Lord and in the power of His might"* (Ephesians 6:10), but those who ignore or refuse this provision while lusting for former things, will soon perish and be buried in the sands of the wilderness—the very place where the manna that they rejected had come down.

(From *Times of Refreshing*)

Diversionary Tactics

"But I am frightened, fearing that in some way you will be led away from your pure and simple devotion to our Lord, just as Eve was deceived by Satan in the Garden of Eden" (2 Corinthians 11:6).

What has happened to worship? Where are the proclaimers that "Jesus is Lord?" Where are those prayer meetings where the flow of the Spirit in other tongues seems to make time stand still and Jesus supremely real?

These were the immediate products of the outpouring of the Spirit we generally refer to as the Charismatic Renewal. The initial thrust of the Spirit was to make Jesus real in the Word, to make worship vital through praise, and to make fellowship meaningful because it was Christ-centered. What has happened?

Today the emphasis seems to be more on structure, submission, sex and authority. We seem to be wrangling over the place of apostles, elders and women in the body. We seem to be more interested in being a New Testament church than in being New Testament believers. How did the first produce the second? How could this come out of that?

I realize that the coming of the Spirit into the life of the believer begins to effect radical changes in his life and behavior. We are not only brought into a right relationship with God, but with one another and with ourselves. We begin to examine and apply many Scriptures which before were grossly skimmed over. When we are filled with God, we automatically come under the dealings of God in order that we may become mature sons of God. But the purpose of these changes and dealings is not to focus our attention on them, but to submit our will to the will of God and press earnestly *"toward the mark for the prize of the high calling of God in Christ Jesus"* (Phil. 3:14).

Is it possible that Satan has diverted our attention from majors to minors, from product to by-product? Satan is a master at diversion. If he cannot prevent you from coming into a vital relationship with God, he will amass his forces to divert you from that relationship. When he could not prevent Eve from enjoying a living partnership with God, he diverted her by introducing a logical premise, *"Hath God said...?"* The moment Eve became concerned with the seeming illogical demand that one tree in the garden be forbidden to her, she traded living companionship for a lust of knowledge and lost both.

Some years ago, I was studying to be a pilot. When, after hours of study, instruction and practice, my instructor certified that I was ready to take my federal flight examination, I lived in animated excitement awaiting my appointment. On the day chosen, however, the airport was closed with fog until two hours before sunset. The FAA examiner and I took off almost immediately, discovering very rapidly that the fog had lifted only over our airport and that I would have to take my exam while flying on top of the clouds with only occasional ground observation. I was totally dependent upon radio navigation. After satisfying my examiner for nearly an hour, he pointed across my face to a pair of mountain peaks protruding above the cloud-filled valley and asked me to identify them. I studied them for a few moments, amazed at how different everything looked when enveloped in a white blanket, quickly checked the map, and correctly named them.

Then I brought my attention back to flying. Something had gone wrong. The needle on the radio navigation pointed a far different direction from the nose of my plane. Although I could not see the ground for visual reference, I found it difficult to believe I could have turned the plane that far off course during the brief moments I was studying the mountains and map.

The instructor's voice interrupted my misgiving with, "Cornwall, are you going to trust your feelings or the instrument?"

"The instruments, sir" was my immediate response, for I had been well drilled in this by my instrument flight instructor.

Even as I began to turn the plane to a new heading, I found myself deeply questioning the instrument. Then I realized that the examiner had challenged me to believe the one instrument, not all the instruments. One cardinal rule of flying on instruments is to scan ALL the gauges. One instrument balances another and often backs up the other. The moment I looked intently at the magnetic compass, I realized that I hadn't deviated from my original course and that any adjustment I made to line up with the radio course now showing would take me off the original flight plan. Only then did I check the numbers on the radio dial to discover that while my attention had been diverted to the mountains, the examiner had quickly reset my radio-navigational dial to a different VOR. His diversion almost worked. Had I blindly followed the dial of the mis-set radio, I would have taken us out over the Pacific Ocean instead of back to the home airport.

153

It was only a test, but through it, I learned to not follow the needle unless I was sure of the station to which it was tuned, and that my safety was to check with the back-up instruments before making radical changes in my flight path.

Is it not possible that during the past few months, the devil has cleverly diverted our attention while resetting the dials? Perhaps this is why we are so blindly pursuing the matter of submitting one to another; wife to husband, pastors to other pastors, and why we are so obsessed with sexual inadequacies and family unrest. Why are we so unduly concerned with the place of elders and of women in the church? Do these signals direct us into safe relationship with Jesus Christ or do they divert us from that fellowship? What heading are we following and where will it lead us?

Having begun to soar in the Spirit, a fog seems to have obliterated the long familiar landmarks and we are "on instruments." May God help us to check our present course against the compass of the Spirit-Word in agreement, double check what station we are getting our signals from, and turn back onto the course that leads us into fellowship with God.

(From *Praise Digest*)

The "GO" In Gospel

Jesus put the GO into the *Go*spel. Jesus, like an "itinerant evangelist," constantly on the move, took the news of God's kingdom to the "whosoever." From the Temple to the territory of Samaria and from the seashore to the mountain peaks, Jesus *"... went about doing good, and healing all that were oppressed of the devil; for God was with Him"* (Acts 10:38).

Jesus not only took the Gospel to the people Himself, He also delegated others to do the same thing. He sent forth seventy appointees in teams of two (Luke 10:1), empowering them to demonstrate the reality of the kingdom of God. He commissioned the twelve disciples to go *"to the lost sheep of the house of Israel. And as ye go, preach, saying, The kingdom of heaven is at hand. Heal the sick, cleanse the lepers, raise the dead, cast out devils: freely ye have received, freely give"* (Matt. 10:6-8).

After the resurrection, the angel of the Lord told Mary Magdalene and the other Mary, *"Come, see... go quickly, and tell..."* (Matt. 28:6-7). Later, Jesus told the eleven remaining disciples, *"Go ye therefore, and teach all nations... teaching them to observe all things whatsoever I have commanded you"* (Matt. 28:19-20). Christ's final commission to outreach ministry was given just prior to His ascension. Luke records His words as being, *"Thus it is written, and thus it behooved Christ to suffer, and to rise from the dead the third day: and that repentance and remission of sins should be preached in His name among all nations, beginning at Jerusalem. And ye are witnesses of these things"* (Luke 24:46-48). Acts one summarized these words in the often quoted eighth verse, *"But ye shall receive power, after that the Holy Ghost is come upon you: and ye shall be witnesses unto me both in Jerusalem, and in all Judea, and in Samaria, and unto the uttermost part of the earth"* (Acts 1:8).

The emphasis, of course, is that we should BE witnesses, not necessarily DO witnessing. The GO in the *Go*spel is far less an order than it is an opportunity. It is more a caring than a command. Jesus did not compel men to do witnessing, He impelled them to be witnesses. As the angel put it to Mary, *"Go... and tell what thou hast seen."* Every commission Christ gave was coupled to what they had seen Him do. They were to say what He said, do what He did, and tell what they had seen. People got so turned on by what they saw and heard when they were with Jesus that they could hardly wait to find someone to share it with. They were not concerned with finding an outstanding speaker for a city-wide revival!

Acts eight tells us of severe persecution breaking out against the church in Jerusalem immediately following Steven's martyrdom which scattered all except the apostles. It was at this time that Saul began to make havoc of the church. The Berkeley Bible translates verse four as, *"On the other hand, those dispersed went everywhere with the happy tidings of the Word."* Persecution, imprisonment and martyrdom could drive the saints out of Jerusalem, but could not destroy the inner inducement to share what they had seen the Lord do in their lives. They were flaming evangelists everywhere they went. No mandate to preach could have compelled them to con-

156

tinue sharing Jesus after such severe persecution. But Jesus had given them an inner strength that man could not destroy. They found very early that a man with an argument is never a threat to the man with an experience, and that pain can never erase the presence of the Holy Spirit. They continued to preach, teach, share and care because they had a powerful, inner incentive.

In my experience as a pastor, I found that new converts, genuinely delivered from sin and divinely filled with the Spirit, are greater tools for evangelism than all the professional programs I could ever institute. They lead neighbors, friends and relatives to attend church and to experience similar transformations. One person who has really met Jesus can easily be the seed that produces an entire harvest of souls. One who has heard the voice of the Lord for himself is a far better evangelist than many of our seminary graduates. The simple testimony the blind beggar gave to the Pharisees, *"One thing I know, that, whereas I was blind, now I see"* (John 9:25), is more powerful than a thousand-voiced choir singing anthems beyond their experience level.

The heart of sharing the Gospel is the honest testimony of those who have had a genuine encounter with Jesus Christ. The average man understands a very small percentage of most sermons, but can relate totally to the testimony of a transformed friend or relative. The one who has deliberately closed his eyes and ears to the religious salesmanship of the organized church will look and listen in amazement when someone in the community begins to do what Jesus did and say what He said. When the Gospel is preached with power, when what we declare is backed up by the way we live, and when our love is translated into caring and sharing, the Gospel will again become *"the power of God unto salvation"* (Rom. 1:16).

157

It is not our intention here to indict organized approaches to winning the lost. Jesus was always fully organized. But the key to His commission was an experience, a life shared with others, not organization. It was not simply the work of the church as an organized unit, but the opportunity for each member of that body to *"go and tell... what thou hast seen."* When Peter preached to Cornelius, he declared, *"And we are witnesses of all things which he [Jesus] did both in the land of the Jews, and in Jerusalem"* (Acts 10:39).

The essence of spreading the Gospel is to tell about Jesus—what you have seen and experienced Him doing in your life. Tell it in your home, tell it on the job, tell it in the school, tell it in the office, tell it in the church, tell it to your neighbors, tell it to the nations. But TELL IT! Some may use the printed page, others the radio or the television, but nothing will ever totally replace the witness of one who has had a life-changing encounter with Jesus. It should be as natural as breathing, as necessary as eating, and as satisfying as sleeping. *"Go... and tell... what thou hast seen."*

(From *Praise Digest*)

The School of the Spirit

One of the many surprises in store for the person who embraces Jesus as his Savior is how little he knows about God, the Spirit world, eternity, or even the Bible. As with the infant who has traded the water world of the womb for the air of the "outside" world, everything is new, and all of life becomes a learning experience. Many years later, that person will still be learning, for even the last experience in life—death—is a learning experience; it is something never experienced before.

Similarly, the Christian is always learning. God's Book is an ever-unfolding Book, and the life of the Spirit is a constantly changing experience. What we are learning now is dependent upon what we have already learned and upon our maturity level, but we never stop learning, for we have hardly scratched the surface of knowing God. *"Eye hath not seen, nor ear heard, neither have entered into the heart of man, the things which God hath prepared for them that love him. But God hath revealed them unto us by his Spirit: for the Spirit searcheth all things, yea, the deep things of God"* (1 Cor. 2:10-11). We do not inherently know the things of God, nor can we discover them through our senses, but the Spirit of God will reveal them to us. This is the key that is overlooked by far too many people. The things of God are learned by revelation; they are learned by communication of God's Spirit to our spirit.

That Jesus was a mighty teacher is indisputable, for even His enemies testified, *"Never man spake like this man"* (John 7:46). Jesus taught the multitudes, His disciples, and individuals. Some even called Him Rabbi, or teacher, but all recognized that He taught differently than the other religious teachers of the day. *". . . the people were astonished at His doctrine; for He taught them as one having authority, and not as the scribes"* (Matt. 7:28-29). Jesus taught as an eyewitness, as a participant, and as a resident of the spiritual kingdom He proclaimed. He expounded what He knew, not merely what He thought. He was no theoretician, but an expert teacher who taught out of personal experience.

When the Master Teacher was about to leave His disciples, He told them, *"These things have I spoken unto you, being yet present with you. But the Comforter, which is the Holy Ghost, whom the Father will send in my name, he shall teach you all things, and bring all things to your remembrance, whatsoever I have said unto you"* (John 14:25-26). The mantle of instruction was transferred from Christ to the Holy Spirit. From the day of Pentecost until the return of Christ, the Church will be in the school of the Spirit, not so much by choice as by divine assignment. This means that the Teacher is within us, not merely among us. It also means that His classroom, tools, and methods are different.

The Classroom of the School of the Spirit

While, obviously, all instruction occurs in the spirit of man (often called "the heart" in the Scriptures), the Holy Spirit often places His students in unusual settings that are conducive to learning. Moses didn't seem to learn much of the ways of the Lord until he was restricted to the backside of the desert as a shepherd.

In the quietness and loneliness of that setting, he was able to release much of the teaching of his Egyptian heritage and open himself to the voice of God at the burning bush.

Similarly, Israel didn't learn much of God's ways until she was led into the wilderness and forced into a dependency upon God for every mouthful of food she ate. David learned some of the ways of God on the hillside while tending his father's sheep, and learned many more of the secrets of God while hiding in caves as he was sought by Saul. Daniel was led into captivity to be taught of the Spirit, and Saul of Tarsus was driven into the Arabian desert.

Certainly the Spirit does not have to lead everyone into a literal wilderness of desert, but somehow He must find a setting that affords some seclusion or separation from the pressures, anxieties, and responsibilities of life. The secular is a far greater deterrent to the development of a spiritual life than the demonic. Over-attention to the things of life automatically means under-attention to the things of God. As a teacher in a Bible college, I can assure you that I cannot instruct the absentees. Neither can the Spirit teach the person whose mind is constantly on other things. Unless we can hear the voice of the Spirit, we cannot be instructed by God's Spirit. When our attention is on our job, recreation, or amusement, it is obviously not on God; hence we cannot be taught of the Spirit at those times. Unless we learn to discipline ourselves to take times for meditation, prayer, worship, and the reading of the Word, we will never get out of kindergarten in the school of the Spirit unless God, in mercy, does something to force us into an awareness of the Spirit world as He did for Moses, David, Daniel, and Saul.

161

The Teaching Tools Used in the School of the Spirit

No matter where the Holy Spirit sets up His classroom, He brings His teaching tools with Him. His favorite tool is the *Word of God*, for God has magnified His Word above His Name (see Psalm 138:2). The Bible is God's textbook, and it cannot be ignored if we intend to pass the course. No matter how great the teacher may be, the textbook is the basis of the class instruction. Repeatedly, the Holy Spirit will assign portions of the class text to be studied, sung, memorized, and applied. Since He is the Author of the text, He knows exactly what portion is needed at what time.

The Holy Spirit also teaches us with *His voice*. He communicates directly to our spirits. He illuminates the text, He corrects our misunderstandings, and He inspires us to search further.

Still another tool used of the Spirit in teaching the saints is the *preaching of the Word*. God has set "pastor/teachers" in the body (Eph. 4:11), and has commanded that all pastors *"be apt to teach"* (1 Tim. 3:2; 1 Tim. 2:24). Furthermore, even the saints are commanded to *"exhort one another daily"* (Heb. 3:13), for this is akin to the older children teaching what they know to the younger ones in the home.

This generation has relearned the power of the *gifts of the Spirit* as both teaching and learning tools in the school of the Spirit. By divine giftings comes revelation, and by divine giftings these revelations are expressed to the body of believers. The "word of wisdom" is shared through the gift of "prophecy" and the entire body of believers is instructed in the ways of the Lord. In Paul's instruction in the operation of the gifts of the Spirit, he said, *"For ye may all prophesy one by one, that all may learn, and all may be comforted"* (1 Cor. 14:31).

162

The Methods of Instruction in the School of the Spirit

Because the Spirit is infinite and omniscient, and because His instruction is so very personalized, He uses a great variety of methods in instructing us. Among them are five that seem to stand above the rest. First, we are given *instruction*. He shares verbal and written instructions with us consistently. Second, we are taught by *association*. Jesus called for learners to *"Take my yoke upon you and learn of me..."* (Matt. 11:29). Intimate association with God through the Holy Spirit is vital training. It is "on-the-job" training. We learn by observing and by doing with Him. Third, the Holy Spirit teaches us by *experience*. There is no better teacher than experience, but she is often a bitter teacher. But even bad experiences can be good instruction, and the Holy Spirit never lets any experience pass without using it to teach us more about God, if we will allow Him the liberty to instruct us.

Another method the Spirit uses in teaching us is *suffering*. In speaking of Christ, the Word declares *"... yet learned he obedience by the things which he suffered"* (Heb. 5:8). Surely if the Spirit used suffering to instruct Jesus, it is to be expected that we will have our share of suffering during our days in the school of the Spirit. What a shame that many of us waste our sorrows, never seeing them as teaching tools of the Spirit. Some things can be better learned in Gethsemane than in the Temple.

But the Spirit does not major in suffering; He also uses *success* as a method of instruction. Every time our ministry succeeds, it becomes a learning experience. Every time the Word of God produces what it has promised, it is a learning experience. Much like the disciples, we rejoice that *"even the devils are subject unto us"* (Luke 10:17).

163

The school of the Spirit is not an elective; it is required. We do not enroll; God automatically enrolls us at our conversion. The pace of learning is set by us, and we determine the level we will achieve, but there are no failures in the Spirit's school. We merely take the course over, and over, and over again until we have finally learned what the Spirit desires to teach, or else we become drop-outs.

(From *Times of Refreshing*)

How to Receive Thanks

The giving of thanks is urged, illustrated and commanded throughout the Scriptures. The Old Testament law provided for thank offerings unto God, while the poets declared that the very entrance into God's presence must begin with thanksgiving (see Psalm 100:4), and the prophets criticized and condemned Israel for being unthankful toward God.

Similarly, the New Testament abounds with expressions of thanks unto God and encourages all saints to abound in thanksgiving unto our wonderful Lord. It even includes unthankfulness in the list of gross sins that would characterize the last days. No serious Bible student would contest that thanksgiving flows from man to God, and that this thanks is for both His provision and His Person.

But not all thanks belongs to God. Our relationships with people call for expressions of thanksgiving one to another, in addition to our thanksgiving unto God. It has been well said that the little words "Thank you" form a key that will unlock the hearts of most people. Perhaps there is nothing that will stimulate gracious and benevolent activity faster than a simple, straightforward, sincere "Thank you." It is a grace to be found among the cultured, and it certainly should be a consistent expression of the Christian life, for its absence is evidence

165

of ingratitude, insensitivity, or a dangerous sense of feeling deserving.

At the conclusion of Paul's scholarly letter to the church at Rome, he expressed a personal thanksgiving to Priscilla and Aquila, *"...my helpers in Christ Jesus: who have for my life laid down their own necks:* **unto whom not only I give thanks, but also all the churches of the Gentiles"** (Romans 16:3-4, emphasis added). The unselfish and dangerous service of this husband-and-wife team caused Paul to say "Thank you," both for himself and for the Gentile Christians. He was merely doing what he had commanded the Roman Christians to do in giving *"honor to whom honor is due"* (Romans 13:7). I have no doubt that Paul repeatedly thanked God for Priscilla and Aquila, but he also thanked these saints.

It is my personal observation that among Christians, the problem is far less the giving of thanks where it is due, for the Holy Spirit is a perfect gentleman at all times, than it is the difficulty we have in receiving thanks from one another. Inasmuch as nothing can truly be given until it is received, our inability to accept thanks that has been offered greatly hinders the expression of thanksgiving among the brotherhood.

Our Relationship With Others is Affected

The way we receive thanks greatly affects our long-term relationships with other people. If, for instance, I should respond to your expressed "Thank you" with a terse "Don't thank me—thank God," I have rebuffed you, corrected you, and maybe even shamed you. My refusal to accept the thanks rejects your offer, and my telling you where that thanks should be given reeks of a superior attitude. In all likelihood, none of these thoughts have actually crossed my mind, but in my insecurity and false humility, I have declared, "I don't know how to receive praise gracefully."

Just a week ago, I was ministering in a large church that has three Sunday morning services. At the conclusion of each service, the executive secretary ushered me from the auditorium into the pastor's study for a few minutes of rest, while the pastoring staff stood at the front of the auditorium to minister to the needs of individuals. During a luncheon on Monday, one of these pastors told me that the previous day a person apparently mistook him for the special speaker and expressed enthusiastic thanks for the morning service. He confessed to me that at first he wasn't certain whether to explain her mistaken identity, or to merely receive the thanks. He elected to accept it graciously and then passed it on to me. I told him that I thought he had manifested good judgment and Christian grace, since it satisfied the need of this woman to express her thanks, it did not embarrass her, and that by passing on the thanks to me, he assured that her ultimate purpose had been completely fulfilled. This brother was a retired pastor with many years of experience in dealing with people. His maturity put a person at ease and maintained a working relationship between them.

When Jesus said that it was *"more blessed to give than to receive,"* He may very well have been talking about more than just money. It is far easier to praise than to be praised, and to give thanks than to receive thanks, but someone must be the recipient or none can be the giver.

In a convention recently, an enthusiastic sister was brought to the pastor's study between morning services to express her profound thanksgiving for my book on praise. She declared that it had actually saved her life, giving many details. She asked me if I would be willing to autograph this book if she brought it to the evening service, and I told her that I would be happy to do so. The benediction had hardly been pronounced when she began marching down the center aisle with book in hand and met me at the pulpit with a reminder that I had promised to autograph her copy of my book. I took it from her hand and inwardly realized how quickly God can prick our balloon of pride, for it wasn't even one of my books. It was a praise book written by another author. Without saying a word to her, I signed the book and returned it to her. She thanked me and left without discovering her mistake. I hope she never discovers it, for she has a sense of having discharged her obligation to say "Thank you" to one whom God has used to help her find a new direction for her life. The next time I see this writer, I will pass the thanks on to him.

Just yesterday, a young pastor confided in me that he was fearful he might be headed for severe chastisement from God because so many of his staff and parishioners were expressing their thanks and appreciation to him for his ministry. He didn't know how to respond to them nor what to do with the thanks. I told him that a simple "You're welcome, and thanks for receiving my ministry" was a sufficient answer to the individual, and that he could easily give all that thanks to God at his next prayer session. It is better that he run the risk of being praised than to reject that praise and offend the people with whom God has put him in association.

Whether we feel that we deserve the thanks or not, we should learn to accept it for the sake of the person gracious enough to offer it. No one should be made to prove that his thanks is deserved.

Our Relationship With Ourselves is Affected

Sometimes our refusal to accept thanks from another is

rooted in a desire for humility, but the truly humble person can accept thanks with little or no problem. This person has a true estimate of himself and can handle almost anything that anyone might say to him, for he knows who he is in life under God. True humility is knowing your worth and functioning within those perimeters without feeling it necessary to depreciate your abilities or efface your worth.

If we possess a false sense of our worth, abilities or calling under God, we probably are living in pride, either positively or negatively, for the person who continually denies his abilities is as proud of his limitations as the boaster who continually parades his talents.

The proud person has difficulty accepting thanks, for he feels that he must explain why, how, and when he did the thing for which he has been thanked. Sometimes it reaches such proportions that the one who offered the thanks has occasion to regret having said anything at all.

If we have a very limited self-image, we may find ourselves refuting the comments people make concerning us. Recently, I was physically exhausted after an exacting series of meetings, and following the final service, I went to the pastor's study and apologized to the Lord for having done so poorly in that final service. I was mentally chastening myself for a substandard performance when the pastor's wife entered the room and said, "Brother Cornwall, that was a fabulous message."

"No, it wasn't, sister," I replied, "I really blew it tonight."

"If you hadn't told me, I would never have known the difference," she said.

Because my sense of failure so obsessed me, I was unable to accept her appraisal, much less her approval. When her husband came into the room later and expressed similar praise, I apologized to his wife for not having accepted her thanks. Regardless of my self-appraisal, what I had preached had met a need in both of them. They didn't thank me for what I didn't do, but for what I had done. I judged from what I thought could have been; they judged from what they received.

It is true, however, that there is a personal danger in handling the praises of men which must be tenaciously guarded against, and that is being motivated by the praises of men. If we learn to love being praised, we will soon do only those things which produce praise responses. This will make men-pleasers out of us, while the Scriptures call for us to be God-pleasers. Perhaps the safest balance we can achieve is to neither need nor fear the praises of men. We are servants of God, and His praise should be more than sufficient motivation for service. Still, being servants of God, we can accept praise without allowing it to become a destructive force in our lives. We should neither seek nor spurn the praises of men; we should merely learn to live comfortably with or without them.

There was a time in my early ministry when I did not understand this principle. I feared any form of praise, especially if it included a gift. I insisted that any gift of appreciation be given to the church treasury rather than to me so that my inner motives could remain pure.

One day a sister with whom I had spent many hours in counsel that had resulted in salvaging a very bad marriage, came to my office with a ceramic what-not she had made. "This is my expression of thanks to you for saving my marriage," she said.

"I'm sorry," I said. "I can't receive it. I have a policy of never receiving gifts for services performed."

Hurt and disappointed, she turned to the door, and as

she walked out she said, "You'll never let us get out from under obligation to you, will you?"

With that, she slammed the door and headed down the hallway.

Somewhat shocked, and feeling that perhaps God was speaking to me through her, I rushed to the door and asked her to come back into the office and repeat that statement.

"You have a church full of people who are deeply obligated to you for your ministry, counsel, and help," she said. "You never let us do anything to pay you back, and so we live with a constant sense of being obligated to you."

"Thank you, sister," I said. "I have been acting unwisely and immaturely. Please give me that gift." I placed it on a conspicuous shelf as a continual reminder to allow people to discharge their sense of obligation through saying and showing their thanks. I dare not allow my immaturity to hinder the development of maturity in others.

Our Relationship With God is Affected

The Scriptures clearly teach that God will not share His glory with another, but neither will He steal man's glory. God is not offended when we give honor to whom honor is due, for His Word commands this (see Romans 13:7). If honor is to be given, then honor is to be received. It is the spirit in which it is received that will determine whether or not it affects our relationship with God.

Happy is the person who can graciously receive thanksgiving from others and in return give it back to God. I have found it comfortable to mentally think of all expressed thanksgiving as a beautiful flower a person has picked from his or her garden and brought to me. I put all the flowers together to form a bouquet, and then when I have the privacy to talk to God without being overheard, I give this bouquet to God, frequently offering it a flower at a time just as it was given to me. I often say, "Lord, do You remember that woman in the blue dress who thanked me for my book on holiness? I give You that flower. The man with the thick glasses who praised tonight's sermon brought me a flower. I present it to You." By the time I have recounted each act of thanksgiving that I can recall and have presented it to the Lord, I have discharged all inner feelings of elation and pride, have given unto the Lord the glory that is due His name, and am no longer responsible for the care of the bouquet of praises.

How can we give glory to the Lord if we have refused to receive any glory? When men praise us, we should praise God with their praises. It clears our mind, restores our relationship, and returns our inner attitudes to a right perspective of our worth.

"Thanksceiving" may be more difficult than thanksgiving, but the receiving makes possible the giving. Let's not stifle the flow of thanks by fearfully rejecting that thanksgiving. Just take it in one hand, and pass it on to God with the other hand. This empties our hands, and fills His!

(From *Times of Refreshing*)

172

How to Receive a Traveling Ministry

In the past few years, there has come a fresh appreciation for the five-fold ministries that Christ gave to the Church. We have also come to acknowledge that the apostle, prophet, evangelist, or teacher is often a traveling person, while the very nature of the ministry of a pastor calls for residency among his people. In a broad sense, then, Paul said that Christ gave resident ministers and traveling ministers *"for the equipping of the saints for the work of ministry, for the edifying of the body of Christ"* (Ephesians 4:12).

That each of these ministers is gifted with a grace of God is scripturally declared, but that each is distinctively different is obvious to even a casual observer. Someone gifted in alliteration has described the differences in saying that the apostle governs, the prophet guides, the evangelist gathers, the pastor guards, and the teacher grounds. So be it. Thank God for the differences, but the very fact of difference means that a local congregation needs exposure to ministries that are diverse from the ministry of the resident pastor. The pastor needs the input of these traveling ministries, but how does he go about recruiting, receiving, and responding to these traveling men and women?

173

The Acceptance

If the formula Paul gave to the Church at Rome is followed, there will be no difficulties. *"Therefore receive one another, just as Christ also received us, to the glory of God,"* he wrote (Romans 15:7). A traveling minister must be accepted as an active member in the body of Christ, fulfilling a calling as valid as pastoring, if that ministry is to be viable to a congregation. Different does not mean inferior or superior; it merely means different. A traveling minister should not be viewed as a novice needing practice, nor as a superstar demanding pampering. The pastor and the traveling minister are co-laborers in the Lord's kingdom. Each must respect the other in all things or they will not work together successfully. Christ's acceptance of them by calling them into ministry must be the basis for mutual acceptance of local and traveling ministries and ministers. They are interdependent, never independent. Neither develops well without the input and ministry of the other, for none is the body of Christ; we are but members in that body.

The Advance Contact

The failure to plan ahead often deprives a local congregation of quality traveling ministry, for the very nature of the task of a traveling minister requires considerable lead time in his planning. Scheduling a year in advance is quite common for traveling ministers, and some must plan up to two years in advance. This is especially true for ministry that will be conducted outside a local church, such as conferences, camp meetings, city-wide rallies, and so forth. The logistics of these meetings require advance commitment before the local committee can secure the facilities.

There are few traveling ministers sitting by their phones

just waiting for a call to minister, even though the repeated contacts they receive seem to indicate that this is the impression many pastors have (They can't sit and wait and go out and preach at the same time). Look ahead, plan ahead, and schedule ahead of your need. Those who feel that this is unspiritual should remind themselves that God is an eternal God Who sees next year more clearly than we see today. Spur-of-the-moment action is no more godly than advance planning, although, obviously, the Spirit is capable of both actions.

In the interest of saving time, many pastors prefer to make the initial inquiry by telephone. This is probably beneficial for both parties. Any arrangements that are made by phone should always be confirmed in writing, for, although all of us have good memories, some of ours are hopelessly short. If the initial contact is made by letter, a listing of several dates that would be acceptable usually shortens the scheduling process.

The Arrangements

Once a date has been scheduled, there are further arrangements to be made. As the scheduled time approaches, you will want to recontact your chosen minister to request a photograph and some sort of biographical material. In this contact, it would be courteous to invite him or her to bring along his or her companion, but specify what responsibility you accept in this invitation. Are you offering to pay for the ticket, or just the additional motel expense? Traveling ministers spend many lonely weeks away from their homes, so an invitation to bring along their companions is always heartwarming, even when it is not feasible.

In this contact, it is wise to find out what type of accommodations are desired; if books, records, or tapes

175

will be brought for sale, and if so, whether the minister would like the church to be responsible for the sales. It is only fair to report the number of services you are planning and in which of them your guest will be ministering. If anything special has been scheduled, such as a ministers' breakfast, a staff luncheon, or anything that affects his time schedule, it should be made plain at this point in your relationship. It's always considerate to ask him ahead of time if he is willing to minister at "extra" events such as a staff or pastors' meeting, rather than simply scheduling it and informing him that he is supposed to speak. Help your traveling minister to serve your congregation at his best level by giving him ample time to prepare. Surprises often produce shoddy ministry; advance preparation leads to excellence of performance.

The Accommodations

Unless the guest minister has requested otherwise, or there are no such accommodations available in the area, a motel or hotel offers the best accommodations for the traveling minister. A time away from people is necessary if one is to be at his best for public ministry. Even Jesus insisted on getting away from the crowd from time to time.

Perhaps nothing is more disconcerting to the traveling minister than to arrive and find that no provision has been made for his lodging. Being driven from motel to motel while the pastor tries to "pull rank" to get him registered is embarrassing to both the pastor and the traveling speaker. It is difficult for him to feel wanted when it becomes obvious that no preparation has been made for him. It is wise to double-check the registration the day before the speaker is scheduled to arrive, and, if it is reasonably convenient, to pre-register the guest so that he can be taken directly to his room. That is a sure indication that he is both wanted and welcome.

Pastors who seldom use the facilities of a motel may find it difficult to comprehend how cold, sterile, and commercial a motel room can seem. There is nothing homelike about it. A bouquet of flowers, a basket of fruit, or a box of candy with a welcoming note attached will be like a sunbeam on a cloudy day. Flowers are often provided for women in traveling ministry, but omitted for traveling men on the mistaken assumption that flowers are not masculine. Still, flowers give any room a homey touch, and although men will seldom purchase flowers for themselves, they appreciate having them in the room. The little touch of femininity that a bouquet can bring into a room is often a balancing factor which helps temper the loneliness that accompanies the traveling ministry.

If it is absolutely necessary to place the minister in someone's home, be certain that it is a home that can offer a considerable measure of privacy, without undue noise from small children. Placing a traveling person in a home with a troubled marriage or other family problems in the hopes that some counseling may occur is grossly unfair to all parties concerned.

In all circumstances, make ample arrangements for eating. Not all motels have acceptable restaurants, and some of them do not allow the meals to be charged to the room. If such a situation exists, a cash advance is far superior to asking the speaker to advance his own money and keep receipts to be presented to the church treasurer later.

Today's best motels are often far from everything. They are placed for the convenience of travelers, not visitors. Arranging to leave a car for the speaker's use is a courtesy far rarer than you might expect. If a car is not available or

177

was not desired by the speaker, assign a person to act as chauffeur for the speaker, and have an understood schedule for picking him up and delivering him after services. I have actually experienced having to hitchhike to and from my motel to the convention site because this provision was not offered.

A final suggestion in the accommodations is to have a typed agenda of all services, appointments, and schedules with home and church numbers that can be called. This should be in the hotel room right next to the flowers or fruit basket. Let the traveling minister begin to adjust himself mentally before the first service.

The Association

Once the speaker is in his hotel room, your responsibility to him has not ceased. Don't just "dump" him and merely wait to see him function in the pulpit during the services. Budget some time in advance to be with your guest speaker. The richness of his experience can enlarge your own perspective, and the vision with which you work can enlarge his vision. Perhaps you can arrange to share a meal each day with your guest. Sometimes it is wise to have other members of the church staff join you in this time of fellowship. This time slot should be arranged for the mutual convenience of both of you. If you do this, make sure this is a pleasant, relaxed time of *fellowship*— not an opportunity to "pick the brain" of the guest. Don't make him "pay for" his meal (which he then may not get a chance to eat) by answering all the questions you've been saving up for just such an opportunity.

Unless your guest indicates a desire for extended fellowship, don't consume his every waking moment. Allow him or her some time alone. You will penalize the services if you drain all of his energies between the services. All batteries need to be recharged regularly. Don't exhaust a person and then rationalize your guilt by saying, "I'll be praying that God will give you rest at the next place." That's what they told him at the last place.

A gentle but honest questioning as to any of his shopping needs shows consideration. To be out of toothpaste or shaving cream can be a real irritant in the motels that do not have a gift shop in them. Even the most experienced travelers fail to pack everything that is needed every time they go on the road.

If the traveler has been on the road for several successive conferences, he or she might appreciate a family situation. How about taking him to your home to share a meal with your family, or at least have your family join the two of you at a restaurant. We all need to keep in touch with the family unit. Again, make this a relaxed time—no counseling or question-and-answer sessions, please.

One further word concerning your association with your ministerial guest: find out if he or she would like some protection from people after a service. Some like to mingle with the congregation after a service; some enter into personal ministry after preaching; but others have given every ounce of emotional energy they possess while ministering in the pulpit, and they do not desire to have to repreach the sermon on a one-to-one basis, or to hear about problems for which they have no answers. A staff member assigned to quickly conduct the speaker to the pastor's office or directly to the motel after the service often becomes a true deliverer to the speaker.

The Acknowledgement

Some pastors explain the financial arrangements at the very beginning, but most tend to leave the guest

179

wondering how he will be rewarded financially. Those who minister to the Church at large are usually expected to finance their own ministries and to "live by faith." This often means accepting a single offering as a love offering for an entire conference. Seldom is a plane ticket, or money for one, sent in advance. Furthermore, it is not too unusual for the speaker to have to use his personal credit card as security when registering at the motel. The church's only front money has been for advertising. Everything else is financed by the guest speaker, but he is often left guessing his financial fate until he is taken to the airport at the end of the services. A brief explanation of how the finances will be handled can relax tensions in the traveling minister, making him even more valuable in his ministry.

Determining how much to give a guest speaker is a problem for many pastors. One way this is handled is to simply take a "love offering" and give whatever comes in, hoping that it will be sufficient. If you elect to use the "love offering" system, please be honest in the way it is done. Don't choose the night with the lowest attendance to take that offering. If an offering is declared to be a love offering for the guest minister, it is deceitful to take part of it for advertising, overhead, or anything else. If the offering is to be shared between the church and the guest, say so. Integrity in the handling of offerings is vital to the life-flow of a congregation.

In trying to determine what is a fair honorarium, some pastors overlook the days of traveling to and from the service and count only the actual days of ministry. Another area many people overlook is the fact that the traveling person must maintain a home, a family, and an office, as well as recover all traveling expenses, entirely from what he receives from his ministry. It is his only source of income.

The local pastor may have difficulty presenting a check that greatly exceeds his personal salary because he overlooks the harsh reality that the traveling person receives none of the usual pastoral benefits. He receives no housing or car allowance, no paid days off, no sick leave, no vacation time, and no entertainment allowance or expense account. He may have an office and a secretary to support at his home base. He does not receive a check fifty-two weeks of the year and he must pay all his Social Security taxes himself. He has no hospital or life insurance paid for by a church, and, of course, he has no retirement program. All of these benefits that the pastor enjoys must come out of the traveling man's honorarium.

What is a fair measurement for an honorarium? Perhaps Paul gave a standard of measurement to Timothy when he wrote, *"Let the elders who rule well be counted worthy of double honor, especially those who labor in the word and doctrine"* (1 Timothy 5:17). That the "double honor" of which Paul spoke concerns the honorarium is made clear by other translators. Norle translates this phrase *"... considered worthy of a double reward."* Williams says, *"... considered as deserving twice the salary they get,"* and the *New English Bible* puts it as *"... reckoned worthy of a double stipend."* Perhaps a beginning basis for determining the honorarium might be double the weekly salary of the senior pastor (and don't forget to allow for non-cash benefits). It may well be that the cost of the guest's airfare should be paid above this.

A final suggestion in this matter: make provision to present the speaker with his check before he leaves town. Promising to mail it to him as soon as the offerings are counted is a withholding of earned wages against which James speaks with prophetic sternness. It is a very empty feeling to have financed a great portion of a series of

181

services and have to leave town with only a promise of better things to come. Too often the check is never sent.

The Afterglow

Usually the pastor feels that he has discharged his obligations when he deposits the speaker at the airport after the meetings are through, but there are two further kindnesses that he can share with this traveling minister. If tapes of the services have been made available to the congregation, it is an appreciated courtesy to send a set of these tapes to the speaker's office or home. He really does not need to crowd them into his luggage, but he would appreciate having them awaiting him when he returns home.

There are a few pastors who, after a week or so, take the time to write a thank-you letter sharing their observations of the fruit of the ministry. This is very seldom done in the circles in which I travel, but when it is done, it is deeply appreciated, for the traveling person rarely gets to see the fruit of his labors. When the pastor will share a report, it puts fresh courage in the traveler's spirit and helps him forget the weariness of his flesh.

How do we receive a traveling ministry? With care in our choice, with candor in the contact, with helpfulness in hospitality, with joy in the joining of ministries, with honor in the honorarium, and with gratitude for this gift to the Church. Perhaps the pungent words of Jesus should set the tone of our relationship with traveling ministries: *"Inasmuch as you did it to the least of these My brethren, you did it to Me"* (Matthew 25:40). Let's receive one another this way.

(This first appeared in *Logos Journal* and has subsequently been reprinted in more Christian magazines than any other article of mine.)